R E A L
E S T A T E
FLIPPING

Grow Rich
Buying
and
Selling
Property

D0048606

MARK B. WEISS, C.C.I.M.

Adams Media
Avon, Massachusetts

Published by
Adams Media, an F+W Publications Company
57 Littlefield Street, Avon, MA 02322 U.S.A.
www.adamsmedia.com

ISBN: 1-59337-018-0

Printed in the United States of America.

J I H G F E D C B A

Library of Congress Cataloging-in-Publication Data
Weiss, Mark B.
Real estate flipping / Mark B. Weiss
p.   cm.
ISBN 1-59337-018-0
1. Real estate investment—United States. 2. House buying—United States. 3. House selling—United States. I. Title.
HD255.W39 2004
333.33'83—dc22
2003020738

Cover photograph © Comstock Images

This book is available at quantity discounts for bulk purchases.
For information, call 1-800-872-5627.

Contents

Acknowledgments

I enjoy acknowledgments, as they allow me to share my thoughts, feelings, and philosophy.

I want to take this opportunity to thank my wife Marilyn and my son Daniel for their love and support throughout my adventures. Daniel, You're It! I love you both very much.

Thanks to my parents, Flora and Al Weiss, whose energy never ceases to surprise me.

Thanks to my in-laws, Paul and Ivana Egel—your support has meant so much to me

Thanks to Kathy Welton and Jill Alexander for giving me the chance to share my experiences with readers. And to Joe Klein who taught me how to flip, flip, flip.

I dedicate this book to those who believe in themselves. To people who think they can do it and actually do, rather than talk about it for their whole life. To people who know that experiencing life is trying new things and that trying new things is not risk, but life itself. To people who realize that you can never win at everything and that's okay. To people who know that perfection is really an abstract term. And to people who elevate themselves by showing how good they are rather than putting down others to attempt to elevate themselves.

Introduction

I listen to all kinds of music—rock and roll, country, some classical, show tunes, and more. But I've never learned how to play an instrument, nor even how to read a single musical note. When it comes to buying and selling real estate, though, I am a maestro. I know value, marketing, financing, negotiation, and how to meet the emotional needs of the seller and buyer. I understand every instrument and player. I realize that in order to conduct a masterpiece of a deal, I must create a transaction that is profitable not just for me (the flipper), but also for my seller and my buyer. If all the parties are not in perfect harmony, then the transaction will never be completed. When the check comes to me at closing, I know that everything has fallen into place.

I was able to begin my career as an independent real estate broker because of what I earned on a real estate flip. The capital I needed to go into business came from observing a friend flip properties, knowing a potential buyer before I even found the right property, finding a distressed seller who was too smart for his own good, having a knowledgeable attorney, and being in the right place at the right time. Since that day in 1988, I have flipped many properties—perhaps not as many as some others have, but as many as I found that were right for me.

What is real estate flipping? Flipping property means stepping in the middle of a transaction. It is buying real estate for less than you can sell it for. That's it: Now you understand the secret of real estate flipping.

But don't stop reading now—there's a lot more that you need to know about the fine art of flipping. And don't think that you're about to receive one of those "buy real estate with no money down" pitches. That's not what this book is about. Instead, this book is about making money— sometimes consistently, though not always. In every situation, though, values in buying properties are out there to be found.

In *Real Estate Flipping* I will give you my tricks of the trade, and I'll tell you about my personal experiences flipping property, along with the unique circumstances that defined each transaction. By the end of this book, you, too, will know how to flip property successfully!

Keep a few things in mind along the way, though. First, in order to be successful you will need to adapt the knowledge you gain here to each individual situation. Second, your own instincts about buying a piece of property are more important than anything I (or any other expert) can tell you. From the location to the price of the property to the risk involved, you know better than anyone else what's appropriate for you.

Trust those instincts! You may get close to a flipping opportunity, only to lose it to someone else because something inside you made you hesitate. You'll find that each experience will teach you something and will help you to identify the right real estate-flipping opportunities when they do come along. Stay patient, use the techniques and pointers in this book, and soon you'll be a successful flipper.

Mark B. Weiss, C.C.I.M.

Part One

Getting Started

Chapter 1

An Education in Real Estate Flipping

Flipping real estate is value buying—buying real estate at a low price and selling it at a higher price. Your profit may be quite high or very low, depending on the circumstances of the deals you make. But the bottom line in flipping is that you make money buying and selling real estate.

Flipping real estate is also usually about buying low and selling high in a very short period of time. This could mean buying and selling in the same day or the same week—or even selling it before you actually own it (see Chapter 13). No matter how long the transaction takes, good opportunities to buy and sell always have one thing in common: the ability to buy at a price lower than the perceived value your buyer has of the property.

Two things to keep in mind when you're considering flipping real estate:

- *It's an inconsistent way to enhance your living.* Although flipping real estate is a way to make money, opportunities can come rapidly or intermittently. To succeed in real estate flipping, you must take advantage of opportunities when they present themselves.

- *The experience will be completely different each time you buy or sell a piece of property.* In this game, flexibility and adaptability are critical to your success.

Two Examples of Real Estate Flips

I first began learning about flipping real estate when I started my career as a real estate broker in the mid 1980s. The first property on which I observed a flip was purchased by a Chicago attorney who went to a real estate auction that our firm was conducting.

The property up for sale was a forty-four-unit building in an area of Chicago called Sheridan Park. This neighborhood was as rough as rough could be, with gangs, drug dealing, and prostitution practiced openly. When conducting open houses to allow prospective buyers to look at the building, I was shocked to see the condition of the neighborhood. Fortunately, the senior sales associate working with me had the foresight and wisdom to hire a huge ex–football player carrying a stun gun to act as security.

The building itself wasn't much better than the neighborhood. It had only half a roof, which meant that moisture and the elements flowed inside. Pigeons flew in the third floor of the building, and the one elevator didn't work. The building also had a notorious reputation because one of the tenants living in the property was a female prostitute arrested for selling her baby for cocaine.

Needless to say, I couldn't see the value of this property for the life of me. I didn't think the building would attract much bidding attention, but on auction night, a group of three people registered as a bidder for this particular property sale. This group hadn't inspected the property at any of the open houses held, yet on that night, the attorney (the money partner of the group) raised her hand at the proper time and won the bid. She tendered her check, signed the contract, and became the new owner.

The next day, she went to look at the property that she bid on sight unseen. Understandably, she was appalled. Her partners, who had prompted her to buy the building, had made many assumptions from the information in the brochure. She was extremely unhappy.

The woman called the office I worked at, wanting to speak to a senior sales person in order to get out of the deal or else get the property listed and sold so that she wouldn't have to own it. The senior sales associates, when told that it was the buyer of that property who was on the phone, wouldn't take her call. They wanted to avoid her at all costs.

She kept calling and calling, to no avail, until one of her many calls that day was forwarded to me. I felt lucky; the buyer wanted to relist and sell this building, and I saw a way to make a commission. I couldn't quite understand how I could sell this building in a way that would make her a profit, but the buyer knew better. She had bought the property for $180,000, and she listed it for $250,000. I sold it for $235,000 in a few weeks. Even though the buyer had to pay a sales commission and the additional costs related to two closings, she walked away with two distinct benefits:

- She got a check for approximately $26,000.
- She got rid of the building, which would have been nothing but problems for her.
  (The purchaser of the property was a rehabber who realized that he could repair the property, fix it up, and supply low-income housing in a community that had a bright future. Today, the property is worth approximately $2 million.)

As I continued my real estate career, I saw many more of these opportunities. The next real estate flip I was involved in happened when I represented a woman who had been widowed many years before.

Her husband had owned a property and managed it well, but the widow had no business acumen. After he passed away, she never quite figured out how to efficiently manage the property. Because of her lack of business knowledge and some management problems, she wasn't able to fill the building with tenants, so she didn't have adequate cash flow to pay her bills, including her real estate taxes. Through many conversations, during which I suggested that she sell the property, we established a rapport.

One day, just before Christmas, she called and asked me what it meant that her real estate taxes had been sold. It wasn't good. She hadn't paid her real estate taxes for so long that the county sold the real estate taxes to someone else. She now had to pay off the person who had bought her real estate taxes, lose the property, or sell it.

The geographical location wasn't great, but wasn't bad, either. I put her in touch with an attorney who could advise her. Because the county hadn't correctly served her properly with the notices of redemption and default, the attorney was able to buy a little more time for me to put the property on the market, sell it, and take the proceeds to pay the debts and give her a profit, too.

The property—a multiunit single room occupancy (SRO) building, in which each unit had a bedroom/living room combination, and a small kitchen (called a Pullman kitchen)—was in bad physical condition, so it was listed as a rehab or fixer-upper. I was able to show it to a number of potential buyers. One buyer made an offer that would satisfy this woman's financial needs, so she signed the contract. The day after the contract was signed, a new offer followed at a higher price. By now, I had a better sense of what flipping was—on occasion a buyer perceives a higher value for property than others do.

I contacted the buyer from the day before and asked whether he was interested in reselling the property. He looked at the new offer, countered it, negotiated, then accepted it, and profited handsomely by flipping the property. This buyer was wise: He knew a quick profit had advantages over renovating the property, holding it for a long period, and attempting to resell it. Not only was the flipper thrilled with the outcome, but so was the original seller, who didn't lose the property and still received a big check at the closing to pay off her debts. This was a win-win situation. In this case, as with the earlier story, the buyer earned enough to pay a commission and the closing costs twice and still make out well.

I learned that people who buy property below market value get great deals. They then have the option of keeping the great deal or flipping it for a quick profit and moving on to the next deal. The lesson of both these stories is that opportunity is usually where you least expect it.

Financing a Real Estate Flip

To do any type of purchase successfully, you have to line up your financing. A few years ago, two young men called me, knowing that I buy property. They had entered into a contract to acquire a rundown multiunit property in a very good area of Chicago known as Lincoln Park/DePaul. They knew that the property was going into foreclosure (that is, the bank or mortgage company was going to sell because the owner wasn't making his mortgage payments), and they knew that there was value in the real estate. They told me that they had contracted to purchase this piece of property and would be happy to sell it—as long as I could move quickly and close the sale in less than two weeks. Something here didn't seem right to me. In a conventional purchase, the buyer requires more time than that to inspect the property and to get a mortgage or loan.

The truth of the matter was that these two young men, who were just starting a real estate career, hadn't understood how critical it was to have their financing lined up ahead of time. They came to me knowing that if they didn't sell the property or flip the contract, they were going to lose their earnest money (money they gave to the seller as good faith that they would buy the property). They didn't have the money to close the deal. Fortunately for them, I had immediate financing available and was able to give them a profit for their contract when I stepped in and bought the building. I renovated the property and kept it as a rental building for four years. At that point, I made the building a condo (in which the residents own their units instead of renting them).

The economics of the deal were as follows:

1. The two young men had put the property under contract to purchase it for $185,000.
2. The man who owned the property owed $150,000 on it. Instead of losing the property to the bank, he was going to walk away, after expenses and paying his back taxes, with approximately $20,000.
3. I paid the two sellers $205,000, so they earned $20,000 on their flip of the contract.
4. I then renovated the property, invested around $200,000 into the property, and let the renters carry the property (that means that their rent paid for my mortgage).
5. I turned the property into a condo and sold four units at an average value of $225,000 each.

By definition, this last part isn't a flip (turning the unit into condos). The two young buyers were the ones who flipped the contract and profited without even closing the deal.

Steer Clear of Creative Financing

If you are just beginning in business, like most people you will probably find that you don't have as much money as you might need. This means you have to use ingenuity to create capital and profits—but beware!

At the time I obtained my real estate license, the state of Illinois required that a new licensee apprentice at a brokerage firm for a minimum of two years prior to becoming a broker. So I did just that. For two years, I began my professional career listing and selling property and meeting many buyers and sellers of property. One of these buyers and sellers was a professional flipper. Joe was from New York and was determined to make a dent in the Chicago market.

I developed a rapport with Joe, and we became good friends. What he did throughout the New York area, as well as in other parts of the country, was to put a property under contract, buy it, acquire financing on it, and then flip it to someone else. He got some cash from these deals, but most of his profit came in the form of mortgage paper, a second mortgage, or even a third mortgage. (He was giving a second mortgage to the buyer so that the buyer could take possession of the property without any cash down.) I wasn't aware of the additional mortgages at the time; all I knew was that every time I talked to Joe, he told me how he had made $200,000, $400,000, or $1 million on a flip. I was filled with envy, because I couldn't believe how much money this man was making week in and week out. I later learned he was not receiving cash—only paper.

What I didn't know was that there was a flaw in his operation. Joe was simply overmortgaging property. He was counting on getting the cash profit when the buyer he sold to eventually sold the property at a higher value for a profit. Only then could Joe get paid off, because all the mortgages had to be satisfied. By putting profits into these additional multiple mortgages, he wasn't getting any cash—only paper. He was speculating that as the real estate market rose, the person whom he flipped to would be managing the property well and paying the mortgage and debts. At some point that person would find someone to sell the property to. But who was the greater fool here? When Joe would sell a property, he would sell it to a fool who assumed he or she could put up little or no cash and then sell the property at a greater future value to a greater fool who would give him or her an additional profit, and so on.

As I got to know Joe better, the stories of his successes began to turn into complaints about his share of problems. People were defaulting on their mortgages, which meant that they weren't making payments to him, and they also weren't making payments to the original seller whose mortgage they had assumed.

Properties were going into foreclosure, and because Joe's profit was tied up in the second or third mortgages (which weren't always recorded), he wasn't getting his money. Just when things were getting bad enough, in October 1987 there was a large stock market crash. Equity markets began to fail, and there wasn't as much money available for anyone.

The poor business climate continued into the 1990s. As more properties were foreclosed on, the profits Joe had anticipated all evaporated, much in the same way that the huge profits from high-tech stocks would disappear in 2000 and 2001. Here's the lesson that I learned at poor Joe's expense: If you flip a property, flip it using regular financing or cash—not creative financing.

My Own First Flip

My first opportunity to flip a property myself came after I had been a real estate sales agent for a couple of years. I had been in touch with a community bank, and I asked the bank whether it had any property that it wanted a Realtor to sell for them. I was just looking for a conventional listing. The banker I spoke to was a little full of himself. He told me that his bank didn't use real estate brokers, because the bank thought it could sell its real estate itself.

As I was leaving, probably just to taunt me, the banker told me about a borrower on a property who wasn't paying his mortgage. The property owner was uncooperative and difficult for the bank to deal with. The banker suggested that I go visit this person, who owned a forty-four-unit multiuse building with stores and commercial space on the first floor and apartments above, in an area of Chicago known as Albany Park. He said, jokingly, that maybe I could work with the borrower, because if I could sell the property I would be a hero. The bank wouldn't have to take the property back through foreclosure and manage this rat-trap of a building, and the owner would happy to be able to pay off the bank.

I needed to earn a commission, so I saw this as an opportunity. When I approached the property owner and told him that his bank had sent me to help him sell, the man launched into a tirade. He didn't want anything to do with me, because he hated the bank and he hated everyone associated with the bank. And as the saying goes, "when you sleep with pigs, you wake up smelling like one." I walked in there smelling like a banker, and the man couldn't stand me. I was more or less thrown out of his video store where he maintained an office in the property.

As I sat in my car, feeling rejected and frustrated—and angry that I had been set up by the banker—a little light went on. I looked back at the property and counted the units, forty-four in all. I then remembered that a successful seller of property had once told me that a building in need of renovation was worth around $10,000 a unit. This was in 1988. And this building definitely required renovation. I knew the owner owed his bank $360,000, but forty-four times $10,000 is $440,000.

I realized that this just might be an opportunity to flip. I knew a buyer who often purchased property for rehab, but before calling that potential buyer, I walked back to the video store to see the owner. The man looked at me with disgust, but I asked him how he would feel about a contract to buy this property that would give him an adequate price. The man's entire attitude changed. "If you're going to buy this property you have to close in thirty days," he said. "And buy it *as is*." I knew that I would have to close fast in order to pay off the man's loan with the bank and not have a financing problem.

I didn't have enough money for the sale, and I didn't have the means to obtain financing, either. And I was a rookie salesman, just cutting my teeth on contracts, contract law, transitions, and markets. I happened to have worked with an attorney whom I trusted to lead me through the steps, so I contacted him. Then I gained the owner's permission to walk through the property with some friends to evaluate the real estate itself.

Finally, I called my friend the rehabber. I said, "John, here's a great opportunity for you. There's a building with forty-four units on a nice corner that needs work. It's just what you're looking for. The price on the property is $480,000." He told me he wouldn't pay a penny more than $450,000, and I knew I had my man. While the buyer prepared a contract, I, knowing that his word was good and that a contract would be forthcoming, prepared a contract for the seller at a price of $360,000. The seller quickly accepted it, and the clock was ticking.

What I did was essentially use my buyer's money to buy the property. I set up a double closing on the same day for the transaction to take place. The bank was informed that their borrower was selling to me, and the seller had made it clear that he was not going to deal with me as a real estate broker but only as a buyer. He insisted on no commission—only a sale—if I could comply with his dates and act only as a buyer. I disclosed on the contract that I was a real estate agent licensed in Illinois and that I had the right to assign the contract (flip it) if I chose. It was important for me to be sure that, if I bought the property, I wouldn't be in an ethical conflict with any of the Realtor's codes that I'd agreed to when I entered the profession.

But there was one more hitch to overcome in order for the deal to close. On the morning of the closing, the City of Chicago Department of Water had to come in and take the final water meter reading for the closing to take place. Chicago, like many cities, has rules regulating the transfer of property that are designed to secure the city's own financial interest (such as the millions of dollars of losses that could result from unpaid water bills). It was critical for the water meter reader to get into this building and get the final reading.

At 6 A.M. that morning I woke, and, disguising my voice, I called the seller's home and told him in a gruff tone that I was with the water department and that we were coming at 7:45 A.M. to read the meter. I actually knew that the meter reader was scheduled to come at 8:00 A.M., and that, with the closing taking place at 10:00 A.M., there was no room for the seller to be late. The meter reading came through. The only remaining worry was whether or not my buyer would come to the closing with enough money to buy the building from me, give me my profit, and pay off the debts of the original owner. And in fact he did

In creating and implementing this deal, I wanted everyone to feel that they had gotten the price they deserved and that no one was being taken advantage of. The bank was getting paid off, the borrower was getting the bank off his back, and my buyer felt he was getting a great deal. (He later flipped the property himself—though that's another story.) I not only had enough money to cover all of my fees, title costs, attorney fees, transfer stamps, and so on, but I also walked away with enough profit to initially finance my business. I even secured a letter of recommendation from the community bank, which was pleased as punch that it didn't have to foreclose on the property. Keep in mind that, in any flipping transaction, the only way to avoid complications is for everyone to feel that they are winners.

Holding Property

When a property is presented to you, you have to assess whether it's better to tie up the property in a long contract while looking for the buyer, or buy the property and hold it after closing for a day, a week, a month, or however long it takes to sell.

At times, selling the contract (that is, assigning the contract to another party and allowing him or her to close) is advantageous. But another method that works well is to buy the property and hold it, renovate it to add value during the hold period, and then put it back on the market. Although flipping property is usually defined as buying and selling property quickly, another way to flip is to buy the property, hold it for a period of time, and sell it for a profit. This method of flipping real estate is certainly a respected and well-acknowledged way of creating wealth in real estate. In properties that I've purchased, I've found advantages to putting money into the property to enhance the value.

One advantage to taking this approach is that after you buy and close on the property, you control it. The previous owner isn't involved in any way, and having full control of a deal is critical to real estate flipping. You have the ability to enter, renovate, or show the property at any time.

One thing to keep in mind: In buying, closing, holding, and selling, you need to find a lender willing to work with you to get a conventional mortgage or a line of credit (see Chapter 4 for details). A line of credit allows you to have the money to close, make mortgage payments during the period of holding, and, potentially, renovate the property.

Chapter 2

Is Real Estate Flipping Right for You?

After fulfilling basic human needs—shelter, love, warmth, and food—making money is certainly one of the highest priorities for most people. Flipping real estate can provide additional income that allows you to improve the lifestyle you currently have. In addition, flipping is fun! This chapter will help you to determine whether or not real estate flipping is the right way for you to earn income.

Is Flipping Appropriate for Your Situation?

Flipping real estate means being in business for yourself. With any business comes some responsibilities, such as properly accounting for your income and expenses, paying taxes, and assuming certain liabilities. And in this business, you have to learn fast and be able to deal with some anxiety, especially when you first begin. You have to find the right property (see Chapters 5 and 6), estimate real estate values (see Chapter 7), be a tough negotiator (see Chapter 9), and prepare for and manage every element of the transaction in order to coordinate a smooth real estate flip.

Good research into real estate markets takes time and

effort, and it will be one of your most valuable assets as a real estate flipper. As a general rule, you should spend about a year on research—look at similar kinds of properties that have sold in the community, speak to an attorney who you would like to work with you, get a handle on the market value for rents that are charged by other landlords in the neighborhood—before you purchase your first property. The more information you gather in the beginning, the fewer unpleasant surprises or intractable problems you'll encounter later on. Remember: Research is cheap, but mistakes are costly—in fact, they might even cause the end of your flipping ventures when they've barely begun.

Fortunately, there are many advantages to going into business for yourself, such as receiving tax benefits that the IRS allows you as a business owner, plus gaining the opportunity to work as many or as few hours as you want. Keep in mind that if you're not prepared to be in business for yourself—if you need others to motivate you or help you focus, if you need a steady paycheck, or if you don't deal well with stress—flipping may not be appropriate for you.

If you decide to try real estate flipping, though, don't worry too much about the anxiety you will naturally feel at first. This will diminish with the more experience and success that you will have. But to become successful, *you just have to do it!* Jump in with both feet, and prepare yourself for one of the most exciting times of your life. The one question you will have to answer for yourself is, "If I do this right, how will I be able to deal with my success?" That's not such a bad question to ask, is it?

Can You Flip Part-Time?

Part-time work usually refers to something you do after coming home from your primary job, spending your time with your family or friends, and working on your hobbies.

Although you never want to sacrifice your job, family, or the other important elements of your life to pursue opportunities for more money, if you're well organized and are willing to spend your free time working, you certainly can pursue flipping real estate on a part-time basis. Many people choose to start that way and end up building real estate flipping into full-time work. In fact, I have a friend who started flipping on a part-time basis, and today, in his full-time flipping career, he is able to flip thirty to forty properties per year!

Can Flipping Be a Career?

The answer is certainly "yes." Many people from many different backgrounds have made a career of flipping real estate. I make it a career, though I pursue other business opportunities as well.

Getting comfortable with the ebb and flow

Keep in mind that finding the right kind of property is sometimes sporadic. The good aspect of this is that every day will be unique, so you won't be doing the same old things, day in and day out. Instead, you have some active days and weeks in which deals present themselves and come together like wildfire. At other times, you may see very little on the horizon. Then, when you least expect it, a good opportunity will become available and, at that point, the action will pick up again. But you must know that the one consistent element of this business is its inconsistency.

Once you decide to make real estate flipping a full-time career, there are two different courses you could follow:

- Freak out when things slow down, and start wondering why you ever gave up your day job, convincing yourself that you'll never be able to flip another property for the rest of your life.

- Recognize that this is the rhythm of the business you've chosen and spend this extra time seeing family and friends, taking care of yourself, and doing anything else you enjoy.

Be prepared for the ups and downs, the highs and lows, the fun and enjoyment of your new career—flipping real estate.

Being in control of your time

Take a midmorning or midafternoon trip to your local health club on a weekday, and you'll see a lot of businessmen and businesswomen working up a sweat. Why aren't these folks at the office? Don't they have day jobs? When you're driving around town during the week, notice how busy some golf courses are during normal business hours. What is going on here?

Many of the people you'll see are simply the lucky members of wealthy families. More often, they are hardworking folks, and you'd be surprised how many of them are working hard in real estate. The profits from their transactions support their leisurely lifestyle, and the flexible hours give them the ability to decide when to work and when to play.

Of course, not working a regular nine-to-five job also means that you may have to do some of your work at other hours—nights, weekends, whenever. A successful real estate flipper is always on the lookout for a good opportunity. You will need to be able to maintain a balance between work, family, and fun on your own.

How Do You Know When You're Ready?

The first step in preparation comes from your ability to recognize value (see Chapter 7). When you see property priced at $250,000, can you be sure that it is really worth

$325,000, as you think it is? At first, you may think you know (but you don't), and you may make some mistakes. Other times, you may think you don't know (but you really do), so you hesitate, and then the property is no longer available. These deals that you don't act on are still tremendous learning opportunities, because they will reinforce your belief that you do know value when you see it. Unfortunately, you may watch someone else get a great deal in order to prove this.

The next step is to build your knowledge of the marketplace. The only way to gain this knowledge is by going out, looking at properties, and understanding the opportunities. This process takes hours and hours and days and days of walking into buildings and people's homes, becoming familiar with seller's and buyer's motivations, and understanding how to put deals together.

To be prepared, you will also need to determine where you'll get your financing and how you'll pay for some basic business expenses. You can find this information relatively quickly. For example, if you're interested in knowing how to finance a property and you're thinking of using a line of credit or a second mortgage on your own home, you can easily find out from your bank or lending institution how much you qualify for. If you have equity in your home in the amount of $200,000, you might not choose to use all of the equity to flip real estate, but you will at least have a practical answer to the simple question, "How much can I borrow?" And "What is my cost of borrowing?"

Is Flipping Legal and Moral?

Buying low and selling high has always been the way business is conducted. So if earning money this way is wrong, then business itself can be construed as immoral. Profiting in just about any way can be debated by people whose life philosophies tell them that this is unjust. But when someone has something and someone else wants it, whether it is a dozen eggs or a building or anything in between, there is a price to pay for that privilege of ownership. As long as you're fulfilling your contract to the seller and the next buyer, the seller is fulfilling his or her contract to you, and you're conducting yourself in a professional manner, everything you're doing is legal.

In discussing morality, you really need to dig deep into how you feel about conducting business transactions. Business ethics refers to conducing yourself in a correct and proper way and treating people reasonably and respectfully, without taking advantage of them. You should be able to look at yourself in the mirror and know that everyone in every transaction was treated fairly and appropriately. Judge the morality of your business by how well you sleep at night—that's usually a good judge of whether a practice is legal, ethical, and moral. If you're behaving in a manner that allows you to have peaceful nights of rest, you're doing something right.

Keep in mind that many sellers wonder whether they could have gotten more for a piece of property. And just about every person who buys a piece of property feels that he or she could have paid less. (Once in a while, you also find a seller who tells you he got more than he should have or a buyer who paid less than market value.)

Some people feel that flipping isn't something they could do because they just don't feel quite right about it. That's okay—everyone sees the world a little differently from the next person. But if an opportunity presents itself to you, and it seems to be a fair transaction to participate in, do the deal.

Throughout every transaction, be sure that the people involved respect you and want to do business with you again. Your reputation is the most important thing you'll bring to every real-estate-flipping transaction.

Chapter 3

Working with a Realtor

If you want to be successful in flipping real estate, you must be involved in a network of real estate professionals. I recommend that you work with agents who have earned the designation *Realtor*. Realtors (also called real estate agents) have their fingers on the pulse of the marketplace, so if you don't feel savvy about real estate, consider working with a Realtor.

Recognizing a Good Realtor

Real estate comes in all shapes, sizes, and forms, from single-family homes to vacant land, from multiunit apartment buildings to industrial and other commercial buildings, timeshares, and so on. Realtors, too, come in all shapes, sizes, and forms, and personalities. As a general rule, though, they all do one thing very well: connect sellers of real estate with buyers of real estate. Because they immerse themselves in the real estate market within a particular geographic area, Realtors have a better handle on what's going on than anyone else.

You should understand the difference between a real estate agent and a Realtor. It's an important distinction missed by most people. An agent may or may not be a Realtor; he or she may just be a salesperson. A Realtor is a member of the local and state real estate boards and is also a member of the National Association of Realtors and therefore subscribes to a rigid code of ethics. That's not to say you can't find a good agent who isn't a Realtor. You can. But people who have earned the Realtor designation have shown that they are willing to do considerably more studying, learning, and testing and adhere to the highest standards in the industry. It's something to consider when looking for your real estate advisor. That's not to say that you won't, on occasion, find something on your own and not require the services of a Realtor. But as a general rule, the majority of your buying and selling transactions will happen with the assistance of a professional Realtor.

Not all Realtors are created equal, though. Some are fantastic at what they do; others just don't have the knack. Here are some of the qualities that make a Realtor really good at representing sellers and assisting buyers of real estate:

1. *Great listener.* Your Realtor should know from talking to you and probing with the right questions exactly which properties are right for you.

2. *Well organized.* A good Realtor keeps track of conversations, and calls clients the moment properties become available.

3. *Integral member of the community.* A good Realtor is so in tune with the community that he or she knows what properties will soon be available for sale—perhaps even before the seller is completely sure!

4. *Many contacts within the industry and the community.* A good Realtor uses these contacts to help you in your search for properties, buyers, and sellers.

5. *Networks with other Realtors*. A good Realtor works with other Realtors around town and across the nation. When you work with a good Realtor, you actually have hundreds of other Realtors working for you as well.

6. *Uses the multiple listing service (MLS) to its fullest potential*. Back in the 1970s, before most people knew what a personal computer was, Realtors used a computer system that listed properties around their local community. Today, of course, most people have access to quite a bit of real estate information via the Internet, but without a Realtor, you still can't get all of the data that's on the MLS.

7. *Tells you of possible conflicts of interest*. For example, if you're looking at purchasing property in a development, a good Realtor will let you know that he or she has a professional relationship with the developer.

8. *Asks questions and listens*. After showing properties, a good Realtor asks you what do you like? What didn't you like? What would you have changed? This way every showing is a property closer and closer to your ideal.

9. *Understands market trends*. A good Realtor knows which way the wind is blowing. A neighborhood that looks great on the surface may actually be in decline. Another neighborhood that appears a bit shabby may actually be bouncing back.

10. *Maximizes the use of your time*. A good Realtor doesn't "tap dance." He or she answers your questions promptly, fully, and honestly—even if that answer is, "I don't know, but I'll find out."

11. *A good Realtor is honest.*

How Realtors Are Compensated

Realtors are compensated by earning a commission on the properties they sell and the properties they help people buy. Realtors rarely, if ever, draw a salary. This makes them dependent on commissions, which means that the harder they work and the more customer service they provide, the more money they earn.

Realtors (and real estate brokers and agents) make money coming and going. That is, they earn their commission when they help someone sell a property and they earn a commission when they help someone buy a property. And that's good. Professionals should be compensated for their efforts. A commission is simply a fee earned by the Realtor for his or her services. The standard real estate commission is 6 percent: a 3 percent sales commission and a 3 percent listing fee (although you need to know that fees are always negotiated). A listing is simply a contract for the Realtor to be the exclusive sales agent of the seller's.

When two agents are involved in a transaction the commission is split. For example, Realtor Smith lists a $100,000 home, but Realtor Jones actually sells the property. The $6,000 (6 percent) commission is split. Each earns a portion of the commission for his or her efforts in selling the home. Take a look at a few numbers.

Price of Property	6% Commission
$50,000	$3,000
$100,000	$6,000
$250,000	$15,000
$1,000,000	$60,000

Of course, the 6 percent commission isn't a rule set in stone. There's often quite a bit of flexibility in any given marketplace. Discount brokers are popping up everywhere. These are individuals and organizations willing to buy and sell real estate for discounted commission fees. They won't be hard to find because they'll be advertising their services in every appropriate vehicle. Don't automatically write off the services of these people. Yes, they're making their profit off volume sales, but so are the full-commission salespeople. What's the difference? Only the amount of the commission. Treat them as you would any other professional providing a service. Do your homework. Research the discount company. Ask questions around town and get references.

Policies and procedures vary from community to community and from company to company, so check out several and compare services and costs. A discount broker may charge a flat fee for listing the property. Another flat fee may be charged for additional services such as providing yard signs, advertising, handling offers, taking care of paperwork, and other chores.

The Internet is opening an incredible number of doors for real estate buyers and sellers and is rapidly changing the nature of the industry. Here are just a few examples. Others are sure to follow.

Help-U-Sell Real Estate (*www.helpusell.net*) offers a full menu of services. Clients can select which services they will handle themselves and which they will turn over to the company. Only then is a fee settled upon. Currently the company claims 300,000 listings nationwide and $30 million in sales within the past year. Other discount companies currently online include: Assist-2-Sell Real Estate (*http://assist2sell.com*), List for Less, Inc. (*www.ListforLess.com*), Owners.Com (*www. owners.com*), and Fisbo Registry, Inc. (*www.fisbos.com*).

Realtors and Commissions

If you're serious about flipping real estate you can find real estate professionals who are more than willing to go the extra mile to help you build a career. It's not that these people are all so kind and generous (though many of them are); it's that they realize the value of working with real estate flippers to mutually earn great profits. I am a real estate professional who makes it known that I am not looking for a commission when I buy a property. I prefer to have the Realtor earn the entire fee and bring me the deal before going to anyone else. I will take my profit from the deal itself, not from the commission.

Of course, you can run into Realtors who aren't so cooperative. I recently contacted a Realtor to get some advice on a property that someone wanted me to list and sell that was outside of my sphere of influence. In closing the conversation I said to him, "I am always looking to buy property and I would appreciate it if you bring me anything that you think is a good building." I was specifically looking for a building to convert to condominiums, and I told him he could keep the entire commission if he would just bring me the deal. He flatly told me that there would be no way that he would bring me a deal, even if he was going to earn all of the commission on the sale. For a condo conversion, he would want to turn around and sell it to a buyer who he knows would then list the other units with him to sell as condominiums. As it happens, I have my own sales team for listing condos, so I wouldn't have needed him for that purpose.

I do know that since I told him of my desire to buy property and not take a commission, that one day when I least expect it, he will call me with a property for sale. He will need me as a buyer in the same way that I need him as a Realtor. A smart Realtor keeps information he or she can use later. I will welcome his call, and we'll probably do business. I'm interested in flipping real estate, not payback.

The lesson here is to keep your eye on the big picture and on maintaining relationships for the long term. In most cases, when you indicate to a Realtor that you don't want any of the commission, he or she will be interested in working with you and will find you something.

Paying a commission
Sometimes a Realtor will bring you an opportunity that does not provide for a commission for the Realtor to be paid

by the seller. One example is if the seller wants the property to be a net listing, which means he or she does not pay any commission to the broker. You, as the buyer, will need to add in a commission to the Realtor. In order to do that, you'll have to pay the Realtor either outside of the closing or at the closing with money that you are bringing to the table.

I have had to do this on a number of occasions. Realize this: In every real estate transaction you are going to be paying the Realtor in some way, either in the form of a higher sales price passed along to you or in the form of a commission. In some deals, you may have an opportunity to negotiate a reasonable flat fee with your Realtor rather than a percentage. But whatever the case, make sure your Realtor is paid for the work that he or she has performed in your service. Maintaining a good relationship may result in a Realtor bringing a property to you before offering it to others. Once again, when flipping real estate, always find a way to create win/win scenarios.

Working with a buyer's agent

In the past, real estate agents in the large majority of cases were working in the interest of the seller (and were paid by the seller). It is now common to work with a real estate professional who is a buyer's agent. Find one you are comfortable with and enter into an exclusive buyer agreement. That way your agent can work in your best interests. When buying real estate, it is better to have a person who is working for you and is dedicated to your interests, rather than it is to rely on an agent who may have other agendas.

Finding the Right Realtor for You

Working with a real estate professional is similar to working with any other professional. You need to find the person who is personally right for you and who understands your needs.

Realtors generally specialize in the following types of properties, although in smaller towns and rural areas, the lines may blur or specialties may disappear completely, because Realtors handle all of the properties in their area.

Residential home sales

Realtors in this specialty focus on individuals and families looking for single-family dwellings, town homes, condos, and co-ops. People often live in three to five different homes in their lifetime; that's a lot of moving around, and many real estate flippers are busy encouraging and profiting from those moves.

Investment sales

Realtors in this specialty work with buyers and sellers who buy and sell property strictly for the investment value. While these Realtors may also work with individuals to locate a personal residence, their focus is on helping their clients earn a return on investment. Any type of property that might earn good returns could be considered for investment: homes, industrial properties, shopping centers, office buildings, warehouses, developments, farms and ranches, or undeveloped land.

Industrial sales

Realtors in this specialty work with properties in this extremely varied and broad market that ranges from a simple tin shed in which light manufacturing takes place to a multibuilding plant with a raw materials yard, manufacturing units, maintenance sheds, shipping and loading docks, and its own rail line.

As you become involved in real estate flipping, you are most likely to work with Realtors in the first category, residential home sales. You might at some point work with a

Realtor in any category; just be sure that you have a good understanding of each market and how it works.

If you want your real-estate-flipping transactions to be enjoyable and profitable, I suggest finding your perfect Realtor and sticking with that person for the rest of your flipping life. Of course, finding the right person(s) takes time, and you may work with several real estate professionals before you find The One. That's okay. Take your time. Skill, ability, talent, and experience are very important, but so is a healthy and congenial relationship. Personalities play a major role in the success or failure of real estate deals. Really get to know the other person and see how good a "fit" you make. Also, never forget that loyalty is a two-way street.

Generally, here's what you want to look for in a Realtor:

1. Someone who gives great advice when you're starting out and knows how to back off as you become more experienced.
2. Someone who sees the possibilities in a variety of properties, those that are exceptional deals, those that are in up-and-coming neighborhoods, those that don't look great on the surface but would benefit from renovation, and so on.
3. Someone who is willing to let you know about properties before they hit the market. That's right— a good Realtor can hook you up with a seller before the property is officially listed and available to the general public. In these cases, you may have an opportunity to negotiate directly with the seller and avoid a bidding frenzy. (Note that Realtors are under an obligation with their local boards to input a listing quickly, usually within twenty-four hours of getting it. In flipping real estate, though, twenty-four hours can be an incredibly long time for the individual prepared to act on a good deal.)

4. Someone who doesn't try to compete with you. (Although you'd think that Realtors only represent buyers and sellers, they quite often represent themselves, too, and may transition away from dealing with clients because they can make more money buying and selling property rather than simply brokering deals.)

In the rough-and-tumble world of real estate, this last point requires some explanation. As I see it, there are three forms of competition:

1. *Underhanded competition of the lie, cheat, beat, and steal philosophy.* I don't operate this way and I don't work with people who do.
2. *Open competition.* I enjoy this. Everything's on the up and up. I have many tough competitors and I can be pretty tough myself. At the end of the day, we can enjoy good conversation over our favorite adult beverage with the "battles" of the day the furthest thing from our minds.
3. *Cooperative competition.* Every once in a while, you'll come across a flipping opportunity where there's a far better chance of success if you unite your forces rather than approach it separately. A good Realtor knows this and is always looking for opportunities to "partner up" with a proven ally.

So, how can you locate a great Realtor? Here's what you do: Find out who the most active brokers and Realtors are in your community, both in listings and in sales. A listing broker is a licensed real estate broker or agent who lists a specific property. A selling Realtor (broker or agent) brings the property's buyer into the picture. (A Realtor can be both and do both, but some prefer one side or the other.) It is common for the listing broker and the selling Realtor to split the real estate commission.

Call those people at the top of your lists and let them know that you're a qualified buyer. Don't call just one Realtor, call several. (Note: Realtors don't need to know that your intention is to flip, only that you want to buy. They will know inherently that you will want to buy low and sell high.) A sale is a sale, but the best business is refined and mature.

You will then need to interview these people, preferably in person rather than on the phone. Ask for an appointment. Don't make it too formal. Just say you'd like to introduce yourself and get to know the Realtor. Keep it low-key. Meeting for coffee, lunch, or even an early breakfast is fine. You want a chance to get to know these people but also evaluate them as you would any other professional. Do they seem to know their business? What are their references? What's their track record? How long have they been in real estate in this area (very important)? What's their workload? Ask a lot of friendly questions and be prepared to answer a few yourself.

Pay attention to that "fit" I mentioned. Real estate flipping is fun, exciting, and profitable, but it can be full of stress. You want to work with people who can handle that stress and who can help you handle a bit of your own. You don't have to become best buddies, but you will need to be able to work closely together and in harmony.

At some point you will recognize which professional or professionals make that "fit."

Those are your Realtors.

Steering Clear of Lousy Realtors

Unfortunately, some Realtors aren't great at their jobs. As in every industry, we are cursed with our share of "rotten apples." Thankfully, these so-called real estate "professionals" are few and far between. Here are the three kinds of Realtors you want to avoid.

Pushy Realtors

Certainly, a Realtor will want to sell you his or her listing over the listing of another Realtor, because the commission will be higher. But if that's not a property you want, you shouldn't feel pressured to buy it. If a Realtor keeps on being pushy, push that Realtor away and find another partner.

Realtors who aren't in control

Beware of Realtors who get open listings, yet don't have the ability to deliver the product. A poor Realtor doesn't recognize when a seller really isn't ready to sell or isn't willing to sell at the price listed.

Recently, I was approached by a Realtor who offered me a fourteen-unit building on the northwest side of Chicago. The property was listed; the price was in the multiple listing service as $1,650,000—a lot of money, but not too far off the mark for such a large piece of property. However, when I analyzed and looked at the property, I figured the value to be below that amount. I called the Realtor to get some information on how much wiggle room the seller may have with respect to the asking price, and he indicated that the seller had told him of a selling price range. So, I made my offer on the lower end of the range suggested by the broker.

The next morning, the Realtor called to tell me that my offer was within the range and that the seller had countered my offer with another reasonable price, and I began to get enthusiastic: I could visualize owning this building and then having the opportunity to flip it. I suggested that the Realtor get a signature on a contract and bring the signed contract back to me as soon as possible.

The Realtor called me later in the afternoon only to tell me that the seller, after hearing from the Realtor that I was willing to accept his offer, had decided to stall for a few days. I was told to call back in a few days. I did so enthusiastically and asked whether he had heard from the seller yet, but he hadn't. He said he would call that afternoon. At 5 P.M., when I had not heard from the Realtor, I realized that the Realtor had no control over the deal.

Why wasn't the Realtor in control? Who knows? There could be a hundred reasons. His client may not have been serious in the first place. He may have been one of those pushy Realtors who basically forced the listing on a seller who wasn't all that anxious to sell. Perhaps the seller really was wishy-washy. Maybe the seller got cold feet at the last moment. There might have been a sudden change in the owner's business or business plans. Maybe the Realtor just hadn't done his homework and didn't really know his client. Again, who knows? It doesn't really matter. The bottom line is, he wasn't in control and I didn't have a deal.

Realtors who don't understand a seller's motivation

Good Realtors know what a seller's motivations are; bad Realtors don't. There are any number of good reasons to sell any given piece of property: an influx of capital, to get out of a bad deal, the company or family is moving across town, business has turned sour, it's too big or too small, and so on and so on. But each owner has one very key reason for making that specific sale. This is his or her "hot button," the key motivating factor, and that's the area on which a good Realtor approaches the situation. Every reason for listing with that Realtor, for marketing the property, and for selling to a good buyer must be based on that key reason. Other factors can be used to bolster an argument, but that key motivating factor is at the center of that sales universe. It's called marketing and that's how you make property move.

Always ask your Realtor why the seller wants to sell now, whether the seller has already rejected offers, and if other offers have been rejected, ask why. The answers to these questions tell you two important pieces of information:

- If your seller is patiently looking for the highest price, and isn't motivated to sell by other factors, then this probably isn't a property that you can flip success-fully. (Remember: To flip profitably, you have to buy low and sell high.) Pay too much and you could be stuck in a long-term relationship with a building you really don't want to keep.
- If the seller has had an offer at a price that exceeds what you are willing to pay, you certainly know the property isn't for you.

Getting the Most out of Your Agent

Here are some tips for getting the most out of working with real estate agents:

1. *Be honest about your finances.* If you have a bad credit report or other problem, lay it on the table right away.

2. *Understand everyone's role.* You may be working with two different persons—a salesperson and a broker. Occasionally they are one and the same. A broker is a person or company licensed by your state to represent sellers or buyers of property. Most brokers have a staff of full- or part-time salespeople working for them who are commonly referred to as agents.

3. *Use your agent's MLS access.* This access to the Web allows buyers to examine many properties from many broker members. Commissions are split between the listing broker and the agent who makes the sale. Your agent's access will save you hours and even days of property research, and they can show you the pricing for comparable properties in your area. You must be with your agent on

how his use of his (VOW) Virtual Office Web site can assist you. Explore my VOW at *www.markbweiss.com*.

4. *Let your agent help you in screening your selections.* Agents know the neighborhoods, property values, and trends in the market. Tell your agent what you want and how much you can afford, and let him or her do much of the weeding out for you.

5. *Ask your agent for information about the community and the neighborhood.* It's part of his or her job to know what's happening in the area.

6. *Use your agent as a resource for other services.* Agents are a great source for finding legal services, home maintenance and repair experts, insurance agents, mortgage brokers, and more.

7. *Be loyal.* Once you have done your research and chosen the right agent working in the right company, work exclusively with that agent. (An exception would be if you look at properties in more than one area.) Let your agent do the legwork for you, and never go behind his or her back.

0. *Do not sign a contract with a buyer's broker.* Most agents or brokers represent the seller, and they receive their commission from the money paid for the property. A buyer's broker is different. You, the buyer, pay a fee for the agent's services. If you must sign a contract, put limits on its duration. Thirty days is acceptable, but don't sign for longer than two months. Try the agent and see if there is a fit.

9. *Pay for the agent's services only after those services have been performed.* This is, of course, good advice for dealing with any service professional. In real estate, payment usually takes place at closing.

Avoiding Real Estate Middlemen

I receive frequent calls from Realtors, other individuals, and business representatives who are looking for someone to quickly buy real estate. Sometimes, these people own businesses or they represent (as a Realtor) someone who owns the properties, and I welcome their calls. They know that I'm an active buyer and that I have the financing set up to close on properties that I think I can flip successfully.

Occasionally, however, someone I refer to as a middleman will call me. A middleman is someone who is not an agent and does not own the property. He has no control over the deal. He is looking to "make the spread."

The middleman will tell me about a great property, and then offer to put the deal together for a finder's fee or some other commission. The problem with these people in this capacity is their lack of ability to deliver. They're not Realtors with a listing, so they don't control the deal. I'm skeptical when middlemen call me, and I almost always say, "No, thanks." I don't want to get excited by a deal that just ain't gonna happen.

If you want to be as successful as you possibly can in flipping real estate, you'll need to work with other dedicated, hardworking people. You'll need to network. My advice is to put in a little research time, get to know people, and make sure you always network with the best.

Chapter 4

Putting Together Your Real-Estate-Flipping Team

Automobile executive Alfred P. Sloan said, "Take my assets—but leave me my organization and in five years I'll have it all back." I've met many self-made millionaires in my time, and many of them have expressed the same opinion. Knowing these people as I do, I know they're not boasting. They're just stating a well-known fact: Success in the corporate world, especially in real estate, is built on teamwork. This chapter briefly outlines the members you'll need on your team to help you with lending, legal, tax, and other issues.

Lining Up Credit Lines and Financing

No doubt you've heard the promises of "Buy real estate with no money down!" You may be thinking that you can pull off that little miracle yourself. Perhaps you can, if you're independently wealthy, though even then your scope of operations will still be limited. But the fact is, a deal can close only when money transfers hands. Unless you're facing unusual circumstances, you'll need to establish and use a line of credit (or perhaps several lines of credit) to buy property. It's an easy and efficient way to make sure you have money available at a moment's notice to purchase property that shows great flipping potential.

Understanding lending terminology

A line of credit allows you to borrow money, up to a specified limit, without having to make additional loan applications. It is essentially a short-term loan that you can use to purchase property and hold on to for a short amount of time while you search for a buyer and flip the property. A line of credit works like a credit card, only you write checks instead of showing your card. Keep in mind that you're borrowing money instead of using your own funds. As soon as you use your line of credit (by writing a check from it), you must begin making payments to the bank to repay the borrowed amount. Those payments can stretch out for many years, depending on how you've set up the line of credit with your bank. Note that some banks charge an annual fee ($25 to $100) to maintain a line of credit.

In addition, if you choose not to flip property right away, but instead hold it while it appreciates in value, you also want to have mortgage financing. This is a longer-term loan with regular, fixed payments that usually last for fifteen or thirty years.

A second mortgage, another way to finance your flips, is based on the equity in the home you live in or other property you own. In other words, if your house is worth $150,000 and you owe your mortgage lender $80,000 on it, some or all of that $70,000 difference ($150,000 − $80,000 = $70,000) may be available for you to use to purchase other properties. A second mortgage can be structured in either of two ways:

- *A first mortgage, with regular, fixed payments for a certain number of years.* When you take this option, the bank gives you a check for the amount of your second loan, and you begin making payments soon after.

- *A line of credit that's available to you when and if you need it, but you don't have to use it if you don't want to.* You begin repaying the loan only if you use the line of credit. This option has a benefit in that you use only what you need, and you don't have to pay interest on it until you use the funds. Also, because the line is always available, you can make quick decisions and quick transactions, which can be important when trying to buy well-priced properties. A line of credit is extra money for any purpose you might see fit. It could be equity, just enough to pay for the monthly upkeep, or to make those mortgage payments when they are due.

I see people frequently using a credit line to pay mortgages or pay the interest on other credit lines or charge cash advances related to the property carrying costs. There is no set rule for a mortgage. This week, for example, I will get a mortgage for a property that I plan on flipping in sixty to ninety days. It was an easy way to obtain financing for me and to establish a credit line with a new lender.

Choosing a lender

You can apply for a mortgage from nearly any mortgage company, national bank, or community bank, and those same places usually offer lines of credit as well. Some people choose a lender based on the interest rate or the closing costs, and while you want to stay on top of these rates and make sure yours are competitive, I suggest using a small, neighborhood bank that's close to the geographic area(s) you're targeting for real estate flips.

Choose a community bank in your area that's willing to get to know you, and avoid the larger banks and mortgage companies with their mentality of telephone answering systems, voicemail, and never having the same person in the same place when you call the bank a month later. With a resurgence of community banks—even in large cities—you can probably find a small community bank in your area. You want a bank that's capable of addressing your needs in a moment's notice. When I purchased my first property in 1979 when I was twenty-six years old, I encountered a community banker who said he was more inclined to make a real estate loan if he could see the property from his office window. In fact, when he looked out of his office window he could see the property I was referring to. He made a good point. The community bank and the loan committee were focused on filling community needs. Remember, "Lending is almost always local."

A community bank allows you to combine several different tasks at once. You can . . .

- Obtain a mortgage or refinancing for your own home.
- Open a business checking account (for your flipping business).
- Establish a line of credit for your short-term real estate flips.
- Obtain mortgages for the properties you want to hold for longer periods.
- Open an escrow account for money you're holding on behalf of a purchaser of real estate property you own.

Sure, larger banks can offer all of these services, too, but they won't necessarily know who you are when you walk through the door or call on the phone. Let me give you an example of my own experience with a community bank. When I decided to sell my condo and buy a multiunit building that my family was going to live in, I wanted my contract to be a strong one, with no mortgage contingency, so the seller would choose my offer and I would not lose the deal. After inspecting the property, I called my community bank through which I had a mortgage, business checking account, line of credit, and so on. Over the phone I asked the loan officer, based on my finances and relationship with the bank, whether the bank would give me a mortgage to buy the property. The answer: "Yes!" That's the kind of rapport and relationship you want to establish with a community bank.

As a result of having that kind of relationship with the bank, I'm probably a little more careful with my finances and reputation than I would be otherwise. I don't want to overreach and jeopardize my relationship with the bank. Instead, I look at the long term and know that if I do the right thing for the bank, the bank will do the right thing for me.

How to Approach a Lender

Borrowing money from the bank is how people are able to leverage and buy property. For example, let's suppose you want to buy a building priced at $250,000. How many of us have a quarter million dollars lying around for such an investment? Banks do, though. Before a bank loans you the money to buy your property, however, the loan committee will require you to provide 20 percent of that amount. In this case, 20 percent of $250,000 is $50,000. Without your own equity, the bank just won't let you borrow the $200,000 balance of the purchase price. You have to have money to make money.

Here are some tips on how to establish a relationship with a lender who will be on your side:

1. *Start local before going global.* Banks and lending institutions are usually grounded locally, especially for real estate loans. Start your search with the bank

that is closest to the property you wish to buy and, if things don't work out, move outward from there.

2. *Have your paperwork in order.* Consult your accountant or financial advisor before you go to a bank, and find out exactly what documents you'll need.

3. *Practice your presentation to the lender.* Rehearse with your spouse, a friend, or your financial advisors. Become familiar with the materials you are bringing, and have answers ready for any likely questions. Remember, though, the encounter will be a two-way conversation, not a speech, so be flexible and willing to respond to the unexpected.

4. *Be confident.* Lenders respond well to a confident applicant.

5. *Be professional.* You should be friendly, but always remember that, even if you know the banker well, business is still business.

6. *Dress well.* Proper business attire is essential for someone working in the world of banking, and when you're entering its world you must play by its rules.

7. *Answer every question with a short, direct response.* Bankers appreciate someone who is open and honest.

8. *Follow up.* Don't be a pest and call every day, but do make a phone call to thank the lender you've spoken with for his or her time. Don't push for an answer to your request, because it will come when the bank is ready to give it, not before. If the answer isn't the one you want, call back to discuss any problems; you may learn some things that will help you to improve your next presentation.

Finding the Right Attorney

Every real estate transaction is different, but you will still probably want to use one lawyer for all of your deals. So be sure to find an attorney who is experienced in many different areas of real estate and can review your paperwork, no matter what sort of property you decide to buy.

How a lawyer can assist you

When you purchase property, you want to be able to do whatever you want with it, and a lawyer can make sure that contract language doesn't limit your options. You don't, however, need to have your real estate transactions "over-lawyered" to the point that you miss opportunities because your attorney wants to include harsh terms and conditions that will break the deal. For example, if you're buying a fixer-upper and you already know the roof leaks, is it really important for your lawyer to make sure the roof is free and clear of leaks? Probably not.

I once had a lawyer who became a good friend and a lot of fun to work with. But he tended to come across as too strict, and that killed a lot of deals. Over time, I realized that no matter how much I liked this guy, no matter how much fun we had at closings, and no matter how many successful deals we did together, what really bothered me were the deals that I was unable to complete because of his attitude.

In a nutshell, when you want to make a real estate deal, you want your attorney to protect you but still allow the deal to go through. A good attorney should ensure that you get the deal by ensuring that:

• *The property has no liens or encumbrances.* That is, the taxes are paid and there are no mechanics liens or other encumbrances for which you'll be responsible. A lien is a charge against a piece of property that makes that property security for the repayment of a loan, taxes, or a mortgage. A mechanics lien is an amount owed for labor and/or materials used to build or improve a building or the land itself. A good lawyer will conduct a thorough search to make sure that you don't inherit financial obligations that rightly belong to someone else.

• *The seller is actually selling you what you want to buy.* Do those fence lines represent actual property lines? Are you buying mineral rights or just topsoil? Is the property in a flood plain? Does any individual, family, or organization have a claim to the property? Are there hidden "land mines" within your contract that could eventually blow up in your face? A good lawyer knows all of the tricks of the trade and can help make sure you get what you pay for.

• *You can easily convey the property to a buyer when you want to sell it.* This is partly accomplished by taking care of the first two points, in particular making sure that there are no problems with the property's title.

• *You are acting in accordance with all appropriate codes, ordinances, rules, and regulations of all governing bodies.* A good lawyer also makes sure you are kept up-to-date on changes in applicable real estate law in your municipality and state, as well as new federal laws and regulations.

• *You meet all your legal obligations on time.* It's easy for a busy real estate flipper to innocently miss a deadline.

• *You're not participating in a crime or being defrauded.* From time to time, people forge deeds and documents or sell property they don't own (like the Brooklyn Bridge). You want someone with a legal background to review documents and make sure a fraudulent sale doesn't happen.

So, essentially, your attorney ensures that you buy the property free and clear and can turn around and sell the property free and clear to the next guy. But a lawyer doesn't make your deal for you. In fact, in Japan, businessmen often say to Americans, "Why did you bring your attorney?" In Japan, the businessmen do the deals; the attorneys only write it up. Have confidence in your ability to make your deal, and then ask a good real estate attorney to review your paperwork. (Keep in mind that in some states attorneys aren't used for real estate transactions at all!) With your lawyer, as with the other professionals on your team, be sure that you're the leader of any deal. You handpick them, and they do what you ask.

I think it's important that you find a lawyer who operates on the KISS rule. I think of this not as "Keep It Simple, Stupid," but rather as "Keep It Sweet and Simple." Yes, a real estate flipper needs to be protected, but the goal generally is to get in and out of the property as quickly as possible. We want to flip the real estate. We just don't need quite as much "lawyering" as someone buying for the long term would. My overriding principle is to go with the spirit of the deal. Basically, I want a clear deed and title and to KISS.

What to look for in a lawyer

Choosing a good attorney takes time and, perhaps, a false start or two. I suggest you start with referrals; that is, ask for the recommendations of friends, family, real estate professionals, other real estate flippers like you, and anyone else whose opinion you trust. Then interview potential attorneys. Meet with the lawyer, ask for a client list, talk about the type of transactions you do or are planning to do, and assess whether you're comfortable with this person. Be sure this attorney isn't so overbooked that he or she will not be available to you when you need legal advice. And whenever possible, use a neighborhood attorney (as opposed to the lawyer in the slick downtown office and expensive clothes). You may be able to find an attorney with other areas of expertise, too. One attorney I use from time to time is also a certified public accountant (CPA). This means that I'm able to consult with this lawyer about issues impacted by taxes. In any case, find someone who will likely charge a reasonable fee, be available to you, and have a lot of experience with the real estate in your area.

You can check references through the local bar association in your community, or your state bar association, which provides a reliable source of information about the experience and reputation of lawyers in your area. You don't want to work with someone who sues his or her clients or has been sued by many clients, nor do you want to be involved with an attorney who has operated unethically and been sanctioned for it. You can also contact the American Bar Association, which has a wealth of resources, at 1-800-285-2221 or online at *www.abnet.org.*

Be open to finding a new lawyer, too, if your first one just doesn't work out. When you resent calling your attorney, don't get along with him or her, feel as though you're at the bottom of the list, or (most important) simply believe you're not being well represented, start looking for a new attorney. Your response to an attorney—your own gut instinct, the same one that tells you whether the property you're looking at is right for you—helps you know whether you've found the right lawyer.

What lawyers charge

The simple answer to "What does a lawyer charge?" is "A lot!" Some bill by the hour, others by the project; but expecting to find a low-cost lawyer is like expecting to find a low-cost doctor. I've seen people fail to ask about an attorney's fees, and then find out at closing that the charges are considerably higher than anticipated during any part of the transaction. If you're concerned about escalating prices, see if your attorney can outline (in writing) what all of the fees will be for your real estate deal, and then ask that he or she not exceed that amount.

You may be able to save a few dollars here and there. For instance, you could use a different method of sending urgent documents. You may find that FedEx is cheaper than a courier, but more expensive than two- or three-day mail service. If you want to save even more, consider using a wonderful network called Prepaid Legal Services, which (just like it sounds) lets you prepay for the use of an attorney on a variety of matters. You simply log on to the Web site at *www.prepaidlegal.com,* and you can find out in advance how much you're going to pay and how quickly you'll receive a consultation. Usually you're led to a local attorney who, for a relatively low cost, can advise you on your real estate flip.

One attorney who I have used for many years is part of the Chicago Prepaid Legal firm. However, I did not find him through Prepaid Legal. You should always interview attorneys, even when using Prepaid Legal. The standards for interviewing and qualifying attorneys should not change.

Getting Help with Tax Implications

As a real estate flipper you'll need constant advice on the constantly changing tax laws of your municipality, state, and the federal government. A good tax advisor is important, but a good accountant is essential.

What accountants do

An accountant keeps an accurate and up-to-date account of your real estate transactions, such as income, expenses, and especially tax considerations. Here are a few guidelines:

• *Look for someone who is not only experienced in the profession, but who also has experience in real estate.* A good general accountant may prove to be disastrous in the narrow field of real estate flipping. Your accountant has to know the applicable real estate laws, ordinances, rules, and regulations regarding your business in your community.

• *Understand your accountant's fee structure.* Make sure that your accountant's charges are (1) in line with the services provided, (2) appropriate for the size of your community and complexity of your business, (3) accountable.

Make sure that you get a complete list of what services are charged for and how much those charges range prior to establishing a business relationship.

• *Get references and take the time to check them out.* Be polite and businesslike, but ask important questions. If you don't get complete answers something may be amiss.

• *Get a list of existing clients.* This will tell you exactly the type of business the accountant is conducting. He or she may brag about real estate expertise, but if the client list is primarily local fast-food joints and barbershops, you may want to look at a few more candidates.

• *Make sure your accountant will stay on top of your business.* Your accountant should continually analyze your business and make appropriate recommendations as to the best tax policy at the moment and for the long term.

• *Let your accountant know that you expect prompt service.* You're in a fast-paced industry and often hours and minutes (not days and weeks) make the difference between success and failure. You want regular contact, at least once a quarter, not just at the end of the year. Immediate contact is expected in the event of a crisis or sudden opportunity.

Accountants and tax advisors are important elements of your team, but never forget that it's always *your* team. Despite their expertise, which you value and are always willing to hear, it's your business and you call the shots. You don't have to be a dictator, just a businessperson demanding the service you pay for.

Learn the IRS 1031 Exchange

Every once in a while the IRS comes up with something that actually helps people who flip real estate. Section 1031 of the Internal Revenue Code, also known as the 1031 Exchange, is an example. It's a way to defer capital gains taxes. It states the property used in trade, business, or held as an investment can be traded for like-kind property. You are required to find up to three properties within forty-five days and to close on at least one of them within 180 days. There are a number of stipulations, among them: (1) the properties must be exchanged, (2) only like-kind properties can be exchanged, (3) the properties can be used only for trade, business, or for investment purposes. Like-kind doesn't automatically mean business for business or raw land for raw land. For example, you could exchange raw land for a shopping center or for an apartment building, because any type of property can qualify for a like-kind exchange unless the property is used for inventory. If a purchaser uses land as an exchange piece or a shopping center and then sells the property later (hopefully at a higher price), he has received a capital gain, or profit. It really is profit to profit, or capital gain to capital gain. It is the tax on the capital gain that gets deferred.

This is a very favorable section of the IRS code, but it must be used very carefully and in full accordance with IRS guidelines. It is essential that you work closely with your accountant on the acquisition, exchange, and timing of the process.

Consulting with a Contractor for Fixer-Uppers

Flipping property doesn't always mean buying property and reselling in the same condition that you acquired it. Oftentimes you will have the opportunity to acquire a piece of property that will profit handsomely from repair or renovation. See Chapter 10 for details on why and how to fix up properties you're going to flip.

A lot of real estate flippers are competent do-it-yourselfers. They enjoy the work and they enjoy the savings of not having to hire contractors to maintain and repair their properties. If that description fits you, you need to consider two factors: the range of your skills and the value of your time. Do you have the requisite skills to repair an air conditioning unit or a boiler, fix a leak in a roof, rewire an electrical system, repair plumbing, work on interior and exterior lighting, repair a wall or floor, install ceiling tiles or make other ceiling repairs, clean and upkeep a swimming pool, do yard work, maintain the cosmetic appearance of a property, and any number of other important tasks? Keep in mind that if you're not very skilled in some of these areas you could create more problems and more expense by attempting repair or maintenance that should be left to someone who knows what he or she is doing.

Even if you have some or all of those skills, do you have the time to handle them yourself? Is your time better invested in fixing a toilet or in finding new properties, negotiating contracts, meeting with the members of your team, and closing deals? Only you can say, but I advise that you carefully compare hard costs to hard costs before making your decision. If the contractor costs $50 an hour, but your time is worth $100 an hour, you're better off tending to your flipping chores and letting the contractors do what they do best.

You'll find more details on working with contractors in Chapter 10.

Evaluating a contractor and the contractor's work

If you hire a contractor to do the work, absolutely, positively obtain references before the contractor lifts a hammer. When you contact the contractors just ask them for a list of references. The good ones will be happy to provide them. A red flag should go up if a contractor refuses or delays in providing references. Move on. Be sure to follow up and actually call the people and businesses on that reference list. Some unscrupulous contractors will list anybody, gambling on the often correct assumption that the client won't bother to check out the references.

Call people, go out and look at work that the contractor performed, and ask whether other people are satisfied.

Naturally, you'll want to work with only licensed and bonded contractors. Get at least three bids on any major project. When checking references, always make sure you get the answers to the following questions about any contractor you're considering:

- Was the work high quality?
- Was the work completed as promised?
- Was the work completed in a timely fashion?
- Did the contractor return to take care of any repairs and punch list items that always present themselves in the days following the completion of construction work? (A punch list is simply a list of items the seller needs to correct in a property before you close the sale. For example, you will not close on the sale until a broken window is replaced, a crack in the concrete is repaired, or the leak in the basement is fixed.)

Making a contract and making payments

Be sure a contractor signs a complete contract with full stipulations for services in relation to the house you're renovating. You don't want to find out later that you signed a contract expecting a job to be finished in a 100 percent-complete manner only to find out that the contractor submitting the bid left out the wood, drywall, paint, or something that you take for granted! And no matter what you agree to in writing, be sure the contract states when the work will be done. If a down payment is required, make sure that it is as small an amount as you can pay. Also, if payments are to be made during the process, tie those payments to performance deadlines. Don't pay for the work until it is completed. When the contractor finishes a given phase of the project, you write a check. If the deadline isn't met, withhold payment until the conditions of the contract are satisfied. Again, there's more on this in Chapter 10.

Have someone else—preferably your lawyer—review

the contract prior to your signing it to make sure that it is complete and there are no blanks or lines to be filled in by the contractor at a later date.

When paying a contractor, be sure you retain control of the money by withholding 10 percent until the job is complete. So, if, for example, your renovation job is for $100,000, and the first partial payment to the contractor is $10,000, you retain $1,000 of the $10,000, giving him or her $9,000 for the payment. If you're expected to make ten partial payments of $10,000 each, you withhold $1,000 from each payment, so that by the end of the project, you will have withheld $10,000. When the work is completed to the specifications of the contract you release the remaining $10,000.

The benefits of partnerships

Remember, whenever you're involved with contractors, the work always takes longer than you expect and costs more than the quote. Those are just the facts of life. Do your best to work those considerations into your plans and your budget. If you go into your renovation project knowing these two facts about contractors, you'll sleep much better at night. Although I am not a big promoter of partnerships, sometimes having a contractor who can act as your partner is a great way to proceed in flipping properties that require fixing up. Specifically, if a contractor stands to make a profit selling a property that he or she is repairing or renovating, that contractor will be more efficient in order to have more to gain at the end of the transaction. If you begin working with a contractor whom you like and trust, consider partnering up to flip properties together.

Working with a Team: An Example

A few years ago, I acquired at a foreclosure sale a two-story apartment building on a wide lot in the suburb of Evanston,

Illinois. I thought I'd be able to take this property and flip it right away. I listed it and got an offer, but the buyer couldn't obtain financing so the deal fell through.

Instead of flipping it quickly, I decided to renovate and decorate the two apartments, and then rent them out. After fixing up one apartment, a terrific family applied for the lease for that unit, and that allowed me to get some help in paying the mortgage, real estate taxes, and maintenance costs of the building. The family consisted of a husband who drove a tour bus; a wife who ran a babysitting business for some of the neighbor's children; and a son in his twenties who worked for the city of Evanston's department of sanitation. Not only were they really nice people, but on the twenty-fifth of the month, the husband would pay the rent that was due on the first. Every month, he would say, "Mr. Weiss, I'd like to buy this building, but I don't have the money." I wanted to sell him the property, but I knew he didn't have the down payment. Then, one day, on a morning jog, I realized that, in addition to a security deposit, over the months, this man had paid me enough in rent to qualify for a down payment.

I called a mortgage broker with whom I'd worked for many years, explained the situation to her, and asked whether we could obtain financing for this buyer if we used his rent and security deposit as a down payment. After doing a quick credit check on this buyer, we knew he would qualify. The buyer was thrilled, and he contacted a cousin who was going to occupy the second-floor unit and pay him rent. That Thanksgiving, the buyer's family spent the holiday in their own two-apartment home.

This is a perfect example of how the team concept can work. As the leader of my team, I initially worked with my lawyer, accountant, and banker to acquire the property. That deal went through, but I had to radically alter my plans because the immediate flip didn't pan out. I decided to renovate instead and this change required bringing other members onto the team. I added contractors, designers, and decorators, all of whom I worked with before, to help me spruce up the place for rental purposes. Lastly, when an opportunity to flip the property came up, I returned to my residential mortgage broker, who was instrumental in making the deal work. My professional track record, my business relationship with these people, and the personal contacts I've maintained over the years with the various members of my team certainly contributed to making this story one with a happy ending for all concerned.

Part Two

Finding Opportunities

Chapter 5

Rooting Out Potential Properties

Before you start your real-estate-flipping career, you need to become familiar with the types of properties that have flipping potential. This chapter gives you information about how to begin your search; Chapter 6 goes into more detail about how to identify when a good flipping opportunity exists.

Driving Around

Where do you start? Drive around (or walk through) neighborhoods that interest you. Choose an area you like and look for properties to acquire within that community. Then plan to become an expert on the area, even if you don't currently know anything about it. When you hone in on a particular area, you start to get a sense of the school system, the traffic patterns, parking issues (do the houses have garages or must residents park on the street, with or without a permit?), and other features that affect the value and livability of a property.

All cities are a checkerboard of neighborhoods, each

with a separate personality that binds residents together in much the same way that a small town does. Each neighborhood is known as a good or bad place to live, with good or average (or poor) schools, with home prices that are rising or leveling off (or dropping), with high crime rates or low ones, and perhaps with restaurants and other businesses that are run by residents.

If you focus on a few neighborhoods in which house prices are rising, schools are good, businesses thrive, and crime is low, you'll stand to make profits on real estate flipping. If you've been in your city for a while, think about the neighborhoods that have good reputations, but still have properties you can afford to buy. If you've recently moved to a new area, ask a Realtor to drive you around and show you the area. And pick your Realtor's brain, because he or she knows the strengths and weaknesses of every neighborhood.

Within Chicago, for example, an area known as Cabrini Green is being redeveloped to include a variety of new construction town houses, condominiums, and single-family homes. If you had bought a property from an owner a few years ago, flipping the property would have profited you exponentially by now. At that time, when the area was full of crime and run-down buildings, people didn't know the neighborhood was going to become what it is today. Whatever your preconceived notions of certain neighborhoods are, find out the truth by observing the area and becoming an expert on the real estate there.

Getting Started

The mechanics of looking for properties is very simple. Here are five basic steps for getting started:

1. Get your Sunday newspaper.
2. Open it to the real estate section.

3. Start reading and circling interesting properties.

4. Begin calling the listing brokers or the "by-owner" ads.

5. Be prepared to ask proper questions.

Even if it sounds simple, it's not all that easy at first. It's hard to sound experienced when you're just starting out, but by following this list you'll be headed in the right direction. You'll pick up the experience you need as you go along.

Don't let any of the jargon you will encounter throw you. If you hear an unfamiliar term, look it up in the glossary in the back of this book, and memorize it for future use. Soon enough you'll be sounding like an experienced real estate professional.

Finding More and More Sources

Once you get going, how do you cast your net further in your search for new opportunities? Here are a few tips:

1. *Keep reading the newspaper ads.* As your knowledge and experience grows, you'll be able to weed out the less desirable properties quickly, even from the sparse details in a tiny ad.

2. *Keep your eye out for "For Sale" signs.* Many signs go up before the ads for those properties hit the papers. If you drive the same route all the time, start taking new roads. Bring your notepad and pencil wherever you go, and take notes.

3. *Regularly contact brokers, agents, and other real estate professionals.* As you develop a network of contacts, get it to work for you, and be willing to provide the same service for others.

4. *Call on professionals in businesses related to real estate.* Bankers, lawyers, accountants, financial

advisors, property managers, appraisers, mortgage lenders, and consultants can provide you with rich sources of property information.

5. *Call on your friends, relatives, and associates in the community.* They're an excellent source of current real estate information.

6. *Check out real estate auctions.* You may find good deals, and you can also use the opportunity to expand your network of sources.

7. *Find foreclosures.* Read your local newspapers, business journals, and notices provided by local, state, and federal government agencies. Banks and other lending institutions are also good sources for information on foreclosures.

8. *Call people out of the blue.* If a piece of property draws your interest, give the owner a call. You might discover or even create an interest in selling. Even if the owner isn't interested, he or she might know of someone nearby who could be looking for a buyer.

9. *Get connected with professional real estate institutions.* You will find them an invaluable source of information.

The rest of this chapter will give you more ideas on how to work with these sources, as well as give you some other ideas on what to include in your search for possible properties to flip.

Word of Mouth

By exposing yourself to the market as an active real estate buyer you are creating an image to sellers, friends of sellers, and anyone related to sellers, that you are a good buyer of property. And the best deals are those that come from parties who have not yet put their real estate on the open market. You stand to benefit in a much greater way by buying property that's not on the market than you do by buying property that has a listing, or what's referred to as a listing history.

A listing history is something that indicates through the local multiple listing service (MLS) how much you bought the property for. When you look to resell at a higher price, the listing can act as a negotiating factor against you because sales agents will know what you paid for the property by looking at the listing history. If the agent knows your bottom line, this puts you at a negotiating disadvantage. So letting people know through word of mouth that you should be contacted when it's time to sell a piece of property can result in great gains through being in the right place at the right time.

MLS Listings

The multiple listing service is a database of properties that is available exclusively to other Realtors. At first, the MLS was in the form of a catalog, grouped by location and listed from lowest price to highest. Eventually, it grew into a computerized database that Realtors could tap into through an ancient form of the Internet. Now, of course, it's available via the Web (most easily through *www.realtor.com*) with a lot of information on each property; still, the Realtor MLS with all the information remains exclusive to the Realtors in your community. While you can go to my Web site (*www.markbweiss.com*) to see properties listed from the MLS and receive information sent to you via e-mail each week, you need to contact a Realtor in order to get all the information available on those properties and be allowed in to see them.

The average person can get a property description and

the details that were inserted in the MLS without restricted information such as listings of agents' names and the exact property address. You can obtain the neighborhood and photo, but unless you are a member of the MLS, you'll have to call the Realtor member to obtain specific information and set up an appointment with the listing agent.

The MLS gives Realtors specific information about properties—everything from the number of bathrooms to the number of days the property has been on the market to the annual real estate taxes—and a Realtor can share that information with you. However, MLS listings aren't always completely accurate, so never rely on the MLS listing alone when you bid on a property. Always ask questions and see the property for yourself.

Web Sites

Countless Web sites can help you find real estate for sale throughout the country, both in your area or outside your immediate area. (Personally, I like to stick to the forty-minute rule: I am usually interested only in properties that I can get to in forty minutes or less, because I don't have a sense of neighborhood growth or employment in more distant areas.) Many Realtor Web sites now provide you with limited access to the MLS in your area. You may be able to search for properties in your region by indicating a zip code and searching within it.

Keep in mind, however, that the Internet is only a starting point and can, in fact, take up more time than the old-fashioned methods of finding real estate—reading newspaper ads and driving around the neighborhoods that you've targeted. This way, you can get out and talk to people and get to know the neighborhood(s) that you've targeted.

Others will disagree, but I'm not a big fan of using the Web as the most important source of information in your search for homes. The Web is a valuable starting point, and you can use it to quickly learn if certain areas are likely to be sources for good prospects. But I would suggest using Web listings just as you would a newspaper ad—you start there, and immediately get in your car or walk to the property to see for yourself. Only then do you set up an appointment to walk through the house for the first time. After that you visit people watering their lawns and talk to merchants, neighbors, and other Realtors.

A Web site can be very helpful in your attempt to rapidly sell the property (see Chapter 13). Every MLS now connects to the Internet, as does the advertising you can run in major newspapers. So definitely take advantage of Web sites when selling real estate, but don't let it replace old-fashioned pavement pounding when buying properties.

Foreclosure Listings

Foreclosure listings are notices that a lender is taking possession of a piece of property on which it holds a mortgage and now wants to resell it because the owner isn't paying the loan. You can pursue foreclosure listings in a number of ways. See Chapter 6 for details on how to approach them once you find them.

So how do you find foreclosures? Because of the strong protection of property rights that is a foundation of our country, for a foreclosure to take place it must be published. It must be published multiple times and these publications must be shown to the court. Publications appear in the local newspapers and law bulletins across the country. All you need to do is access the papers and look in the legal notice section. You will be surprised to see how many properties are listed each week. The numbers increase and decrease depending on the economy, but you are always likely to find some foreclosure opportunities.

Among the published legal notices, you are also likely to find advertisements for publications that you can subscribe to that consolidate legal notices of foreclosures from various sources and make them easier to read. Most of these publications can be mailed or e-mailed to you.

Of course, another option for finding just about anything is the Internet. Just go to a search engine such as *Google.com* and enter the words "real estate foreclosures" to see what publications and services come up. These companies are ever changing and the most current information is always online.

Estate Sales and Auctions

So where do you find information about estate sales? In the newspapers, of course. By publishing notices of estate sales, the sellers of property accomplish two things. First, they create competition so they can receive more money; and second, they satisfy the requirement of many trusts, estates, and courts that the public be made aware of the sale, ensuring that the sale is not a closed sale or an insider deal.

Here is another way to find out about estate sales. Go to your probate courtrooms in your local courthouse. You will find estates that require liquidation are often discussed in front of a judge. If an aging infirmed person becomes a ward of the state, that person's home will have to be sold in order for the state to recoup some of its outlay. If you go to court, often you will enter the open window of opportunity.

Now how do you find auctions? Well the answer to this is quite easy, too. Every newspaper in every major city has an auction mart. Auctions have become so popular that in every newspaper across the county—including the *Wall Street Journal, USA Today,* and on down—you will find in the classified section either specific "Auction" listings or else, interspersed in the real estate section, vast lists of real estate as well as personal-property auctions taking place each week. Internet auctions are becoming more popular as well. The online auction eBay sells properties on the Web, but so does HUD (the U.S. Department of Housing and Urban Development). A quick Web search of the words "real estate auctions" will yield a multitude of sites.

Be sure to carefully read the rules of online bidding, and remember that you still have to follow the basics: See each property you want to buy and inspect it first before you become the high bidder. If you cannot see a property in person, my advice is to pass on it. Don't buy anything without inspecting it first.

Chapter 6

Identifying the Best Flipping Opportunities

lipping is about being in the right place at the right time. If you've been following the real estate market in your area, you can find good flipping opportunities. This chapter discusses three such opportunities: when the seller needs liquidity, when the property is near foreclosure, and when the seller thinks he or she is taking advantage of you.

When the Seller Needs Liquidity

Liquidity refers to the ability to readily convert an asset into cash. Some people are property poor, which means that they don't have any ready cash that they can spend, but they do have a home that, when sold, would provide them with cash. If you have your financing lined up before you start looking for flipping opportunities (see Chapter 4), you can create liquidity for your seller and find a good flipping opportunity.

When relatives hold an estate sale

Estate sales usually take place when the owner dies, and the heirs (children, other relatives, or a charity) end up owning a piece of real estate that they don't want or can't keep because of the geographic location of the property. Sometimes, estate sales occur because the owner is not capable of taking care of himself or herself physically or mentally. Regardless, the family needs to sell the house quickly, either to pay off the mortgage, pay taxes, pay funeral expenses, or pay for a nursing home or other care.

Estate sales come in a variety of forms. In fact, you may think of an estate sale as simply a sale of a home's furnishings, art, and jewelry. That's certainly one form of an estate sale, but estate sales are also often about selling the estates themselves! The estate may have been the primary residence of the person who passed away or may have been a business property or investment property.

Estate sales range from auctions (with a judge acting as an auctioneer) to regular real estate sales through a Realtor, in which you go in and make your highest and best offer, negotiate the best you can, and buy the real estate. The difference between an estate sale and any other real estate sale is that the person or trust that inherited the property has to sell it, so the seller is far more motivated than other sellers may be.

Look for the term "estate sale" in the newspaper and see how you can be the person who helps a family that needs liquidity, and make a tidy profit for yourself in the process.

When property is auctioned

Auctions bring in many opportunities to an active buyer. When the economy is tough, people and businesses need money and auctions take place to create liquidity quickly. Many times auctions are conducted by lending institutions after they own a portfolio of property when they need to rapidly create liquidity (basically, when people default on their mortgage obligations in a tough economy and the bank has to dispose of the property). There are auctions for private individuals who need to create liquidity by selling their property. There are auctions by developers who have built new homes, town homes, and condominiums and need to get out from under the gun of owning the property at a time when they are unable to afford the expenses of maintaining this real estate.

Whatever the case may be, when you acquire property at a real estate auction you should make sure in no uncertain terms that you are familiar with the neighborhood and community before you choose to bid on the property. If you are going to buy a property at auction in order to flip property, you must also set your limit on bidding and be sure you don't exceed that limit—no matter how tempting the auction is.

You can find out about auctions by looking in the newspapers under the "Auctions" section. Newspapers are far and away the best source of advertising for this type of sale. Call the phone number listed in the paper (or go to the Web site, if one is given) and follow the instructions that the auctioneer gives. Typically, you are able to inspect the property at specific times and, if you decide that you like the property, obtain a bidders' package that includes the following:

- The date of the auction
- A standard contract to be used
- The title report
- A survey of any income and expense information
- Disclosures and the rules of the earnest money deposits required
- The expected closing date

Review the package of information carefully and ask questions when you view the property so that you can clearly grasp your obligation if your bid is accepted. Each auction is different so don't make assumptions based on any other auction in which you've participated.

Auctions can be conducted under various rules:

- An *absolute auction* is one in which the property will be sold to the highest bidder, regardless of how low or high that price ends up being.
- An *opening minimum bid auction* is one in which a property will be sold for no less than that opening minimum bid, but may also sell for much more.
- An *auction with reserve* means that the seller reserves the right to accept or reject a bid at the auction and doesn't have to sell the property at all if the prices are too low.

Auctions usually work as follows:

1. *The property is open for inspection for two or three days.* During this time, you will inspect the real estate and receive a bidder's package. The bidder's package gives you a contract and information about the house so that you can make an educated decision on or before the auction day. Within the bidder's package, there will usually be a copy of the survey, the title report, the contract to use upon sale, neighborhood and community information, deed restrictions, possibly an environmental audit, a rent roll (a list of existing units in the property, the name of the tenant who occupies the unit, the amount of the rent, the amount of the security deposit being held, the lease start date, and the lease termination date), the real estate tax bill, and other items that may be pertinent to the specific property that you are looking at. By reviewing all of this information prior to the bid date, the only thing that you will need to worry about is buying the property at your price.

2. *You come to the auction with a cashier's check made*

payable to yourself for the amount indicated in the bidder's package. This check will be tendered to the auctioneer if you're the highest bidder. (Note that most auctions require that you arrange financing well in advance of the auction date, and also require that if you're the highest bidder, you sign the contract and close the sale.) As the highest bidder, you must increase the earnest money to 10 percent of the bid price within a very short period of time after the auction—whatever the contract stipulates.

Picture ten parties going into an auction. If a check is lost, it can't be cashed by anyone other than the payee. If you are the payee and you are *not* the high bidder, it allows you to easily redeposit your check with little to no problem. If you become the highest bidder, at that moment you endorse the check you brought to the auctioneer, then within three to five days, the buyer would increase the money to an amount usually equal to 10 percent of the price.

3. *You close according to the contract, anywhere from a week to sixty days later.* The auction contract will have told you when you will be required to close on the sale. (Be sure to read your material prior to going to the auction so that you know when your additional funds will be required.) When you close, your funds must be in the form of a cashier's or certified check, because most auction contracts don't allow you the time to get a mortgage.

One of the major advantages of an auction for sellers is that sales close much faster than usual. This means that the seller gets fast money, but it also means that you can buy the property at a discount and sell it quickly. Just keep in mind that "winning" is not about paying the highest price for the property; in fact, you win when you pay a very low price. Set your limit for where you'd like to pay and don't exceed that standard. Don't get caught up in a bidding war and overpay for property that you want to flip. Your profit is in buying it cheap enough to flip it. Walk away if the bidding gets too high.

When a Foreclosure Is Imminent

Foreclosures present themselves in a number of ways, but it usually means one thing: A lender isn't being paid for a mortgage and has taken the property back from the borrower. Keep in mind that the borrower used the real estate as collateral to secure the mortgage, and the property was that collateral. But most people have equity in their property, which means that they don't owe the lender 100 percent of the value of the property. The lender simply wants to get the amount of the property that it lent to the owner, so it may sell the property for anywhere from 50 to 90 percent of its value, depending on how much equity the owner had in it.

Finding out about foreclosures in advance of the sale is critical (see Chapter 5 for more on this). But be sure you do a title search before making an offer, and research the property for back taxes and liens in order to find out what problems you may inherit. You can buy foreclosures in two ways:

1. Find out who the lender is and wait until it forecloses on the property. Once the lender forecloses, if it is the high bidder at the sheriff's sale (or the only bidder, for that matter), the sale will wipe out all liens other than taxes. In this way, the lender owns the property and can sell it to you free and clear of encumbrances.

2. Go to the sheriff's sale or foreclosure sale within your own community and bid as if you were at an auction. If you buy property at the sheriff's sale, then the sale may or may not eliminate any

mechanics and utility liens (depending on the state you're in), and you will usually be responsible for paying any delinquent real estate taxes that go with the property.

The terms of a foreclosure sale are most often as follows:

1. You bring with you a cashier's or certified check equal to 10 percent of the price of the property so that you can put that up as a nonrefundable deposit immediately after being recognized as the buyer or high bidder.
2. You return within twenty-four hours and pay for the real estate in full.
3. Two or three weeks later, the sale is confirmed by a judge in open court, and you receive the deed to the property.

Foreclosures are a good way for you to buy property and put it back on the market for a quick and easy flip and transaction.

Buying from the owner before foreclosure

When someone knows that his or her house is about to be foreclosed on by a lender (for any number of reasons, including losing a job, being ill and not being able to work, getting a divorce, and so on), that person is motivated to sell. This is because when a lender forecloses on a house, the owner gets nothing except a bad credit report. The lender doesn't sell the property for what it's worth and give the profits to the owner—that would make lenders into nothing more than convenient real estate agents! Instead, the lender sells the property for what it needs to get out of it, and the owner walks away with no house, no money, and no prospect of buying another house anytime soon.

A better situation is for you to get involved before the

lender forecloses. You approach the owner before the fore-closure and offer a price somewhere between what's owed on it and what it's actually worth. The owner gets to pay off the mortgage and any other debts (including taxes), keep some cash, and have a better chance at buying another house someday. Although you'll pay a little more than you would if you waited for the foreclosure sale, you also won't have the competition you would have at a foreclosure.

Foreclosure reports are published throughout the country and often appear as public notices in your local newspapers. If you read that a particular piece of property is going to be foreclosed on, you can approach the owner and make an offer. If you can guarantee that he or she will walk away with a few dollars in his or her pocket, and you can still flip the property for a profit, you have a good opportunity to help this person and make a profit, too. That's a good situation all around.

Before taking this approach, just make sure you research the project and establish your knowledge of prop-erty values in the particular area. You don't want to end up helping people but losing money, or you won't be able to help people for very long.

Buying from the lender before foreclosure

Lenders (banks, mortgage companies, insurance com-panies, and so on) must publish notices of pending foreclo-sures. By publishing the notice, usually in your local newspaper, the lender is satisfying the legal requirement of serving the borrower with adequate notice of the foreclo-sure. When you see this notice, you may be able to buy the note and mortgage—that's the term for the paperwork that a borrower signs, obligating the borrower to repay the loan—from the lender before the actual foreclosure takes place.

Sometimes the lender will sell the note and mortgage at a discount (for example, you may be able to buy a $100,000 note and mortgage for $75,000), and sometimes the lender will want the full amount. If you do acquire the mortgage note, you become the lender: Your money is tied up, so you need to carry through with the foreclosure sale in order to own and then sell the property.

Lenders may or may not choose to sell their notes at a discount; that is something that needs to be negotiated with them. In order to buy a note prior to a mortgage foreclosure sale, you have to do a couple of things. First, you need to have the cash to close and buy the note. Second, you need to make sure that you are well aware of all of the obligations that come with that note. Those obligations could be back taxes, mechanics liens, or other items of financial obligation.

It is essential to have an attorney working with you who is familiar with reviewing foreclosure documents and with the details of foreclosure, title, and other items. All too often I see banks that allow borrowers to hand them back properties in something called a deed in lieu of foreclosure. Often the bank officers who accept the deed in lieu don't understand how the deed in lieu process works, and they end up with many obligations from a bad borrower that they now have to deal with. These obligations could often be wiped out and avoided by going through a foreclosure sale.

Foreclosure Transactions: Two Examples

Here's one example of how this process can work. A few years ago, a friend who was managing a property for an out-of-state lender called me and asked whether I was interested in buying the note on that property. The lender owned a small building in an area of Chicago known as Logan Square. The building had a mortgage, but the lender wanted out of this property and agreed to a big discount on the note and mortgage. Why would it discount the note and mortgage and sell them at a loss? Well, the lender thought the property might have had some environmental problem like an underground fuel or heating oil storage tank. I signed a letter of intent to purchase the property and then took my time to explore this potential hazard, which I found did not exist. I was lucky because the lender wanted to sell this note and just get it off of its books.

The lender was willing to take almost a 50 percent discount, which is exactly like buying a dollar for fifty cents! I knew I had two options:

1. *Proceed with the sheriff's sale.* If someone bid the note amount at the sheriff's sale, I stood to make a nice profit in a relatively short period of time. This is known as flipping the note and is discussed in detail in Chapter 14.
2. *Don't proceed with the sheriff's sale.* Keep the property, if only temporarily, and flip the property.

So, I could flip the note or flip the building, and either is a wonderful opportunity. I consulted with my attorney who reviewed the minutes of foreclosure (the official record of the foreclosure proceedings that tells you what's been going on with this foreclosure), title report (which makes sure that no one else besides the lender has a claim to the property), and other documents to find out if I could acquire this note without any liability. I had a line of credit to use to pay for the note, so that's the route I decided to take. After acquiring the note from the lender, I then became the lender myself and I got to set the initial bid (the lender always gets to do this) and make a tidy profit.

If you're trying to decide which approach is better (flipping a note or flipping a piece of property), my opinion is that, when you're starting out, you're better off acquiring property that has already been foreclosed upon (not the note) so that the lending institution can deliver the property free of any title defects.

Keep in mind that by contacting a lender prior to a

foreclosure sale, you're establishing a relationship with the lender. While this particular property may still be sold at a sale to someone else, that lender may have other property that it needs to liquidate in the future, and by contacting the lender, you become a resource for the sale of those future properties. Sometime in the future—perhaps when the economy is weak and the lender is motivated to make a quick sale—you'll be in a position to make a good deal.

Here's another example of how this process can work. Just a few years ago, I read about a piece of property that was being foreclosed upon by a Canadian bank with branches in Chicago. A complication prohibited me from acquiring the note and mortgage on the property before the foreclosure sale, but I bid at the sheriff's sale and was the successful bidder, and then flipped the property at a nice profit approximately ninety days later.

While I was pursuing this property, because I was now familiar with the bank officer, the bank told me about another property in an area on the south side of Chicago near the University of Chicago. It was an area that I had never thought to investigate, but it was in a growth area. The bank had just foreclosed on a twenty-four-apartment building, and the property was in pretty good physical condition: It had been renovated with new windows, a new roof, and new electrical wiring. I was offered the property at a price of $20,000 a unit ($480,000 total).

I called a friend, the vice president of a bank in this community, and I asked him whether he would drive out to the property with me, look at the building, and tell me what he thought the property was worth. When he saw it, he was incredibly enthusiastic about it, and his excitement really drove me to acquire the property. Based upon the income he predicted, the property would appraise at approximately $750,000 (see Chapter 7 for more on appraisals). I had the financing in place, so I met the Canadian bank's price for a cash deal, borrowing 100 percent of the money on credit lines I had established years earlier. I came to the closing table with certified checks for more than $480,000. I knew I had to pay attorney's fees and other costs, so my debt on the property was closer to $490,000, but that was okay.

Sixty days after I closed, I went to the community bank where I knew the vice president and submitted the property for a refinance of the existing debt based upon the appraised value. The bank was willing to lend me 80 percent of appraised value of the property of $750,000, or $600,000, but I chose to get a mortgage for $490,000, rent out all of the units, and generate very strong monthly income. I could also have flipped the property for closer to $750,000 and made a tidy profit. And this was all because I had established a relationship with the bank.

To undertake the completion of a foreclosure is pretty complex, but as you become more experienced, you can definitely undertake this process.

When the Seller Thinks He or She Is Taking Advantage of You

Certain types of people like to play a game called win-lose, in which they win and other people lose. In other words, they must feel as though they have beaten you up. (I prefer to play the win-win game, in which everybody walks away feeling good.) When you encounter this type of seller, you need to convince him or her that you've lost in order to make the seller feel good. When I know the seller is playing win-lose with me, I play right into the deal. I let the seller think he or she has taken advantage of me. After all, I'm getting a good deal, so why should I care what others think?

This sort of person wants to "get" you by selling to you at what he or she perceives is the highest market price (see Chapter 7 for more on perception of values), even though you know that you're getting it at a reasonable price. If you don't play this seller's game and you try to persuade the seller to lower the price, the deal isn't going to happen. So, if you're sure you're getting a great value, play the part and do whatever the seller wants. Of course, if you aren't getting a great deal, walk away and forget about the property.

One time, a broker brought to my attention a forty-four-unit rooming house that originally had been a beautiful six-unit apartment building near Wrigley Field. The seller was fed up with this property. His property manager was unscrupulous and he wanted out. He was a tough businessman, but his business was manufacturing, not real estate.

I knew the potential of the property, because many buildings of this type had been gutted and renovated into condominiums, so the opportunity to make money was excellent. The seller came up with a price that I knew wasn't as low as I could probably get, but it was still a good price. I also knew this guy was an angry man who yelled and screamed to get his way. Knowing this, I prodded him for a little over a month of negotiating, and in every case I backed down and let him think he had gotten the better of me. During this time, however, I had asked for permission to do an environmental audit on the property to check for underground storage tanks. This bought me an additional sixty days, and he was okay with that because, in his mind, he was "winning" the negotiations. During this time, I began to market the property to potential buyers to see whether my theory of what the property was worth was accurate. Asking for the environmental audit (which I knew would prove negative) also allowed me to inspect the property whenever I needed to, which gave me access to show the property to prospective buyers. When the right buyer came along, I knew I had a property to flip. The seller felt good because he thought he had beaten me up. I closed both sales on the same day. It was a win-win situation, even though the seller thought it was win-lose. I won a nice profit without ever taking possession of the property!

Part Three

Buying Properties

Chapter 7

Valuing Property Before You Buy

Real estate professionals use a variety of tools to value property. I explain them in this chapter because these tools can help you get a ballpark value for a piece of property. However, valuing real estate is often unscientific, which means that your experience and gut feel can mean more than any professional appraisal. So, in this chapter, I'll also help you better understand how to trust your gut.

Recognizing How Real Estate Gains Value

Real estate doesn't gain value in the way that stocks do. Instead, real estate usually maintains its value, and then increases in value incrementally, year after year. With time, however, many properties increase in value an amazing amount. Of course, this increase in value doesn't always happen, especially in areas where people don't want to live. Keep in mind that no matter how cheaply you're able to buy real estate, if you can't sell it for more, you can't flip it.

Real estate gains value because one person needs to

sell and another wants to buy—the law of supply and demand. As a flipper, you're looking for one home that is well priced because the seller needs to close a deceased relative's estate, is getting divorced, is moving to another city, has lost a job, or any other factor that makes selling an urgent matter. You're looking for the seller who will take less for an immediate sale. You're also looking for property that has potential that's hidden because the property needs updating or improving. Often, a home being sold by an elderly couple hasn't been taken care of by today's standards, thus providing you an opportunity to buy a fixer-upper at a discount, and turn it around and sell it at a discount.

While real estate appreciates, on average, about 4 percent per year, that's not really the value you're looking for when flipping real estate. Instead, you want to buy a property for 20, 30, or 40 percent less than what it's worth, and then turn around and sell it for 100 percent of its value. So, the value any property will increase is based on the deal you're able to get and whether a buyer wants the property you're trying to sell.

In many cases, the best flipping opportunity is to buy property from a frustrated owner, someone who is tired of his or her real estate. The owner is tired of . . .

- Fixing it up and repairing it, which can drain both finances and emotions.
- Dealing with taxes; after all, you can't beat city hall, especially if the owner has gotten into a rift with a local councilperson and now is perpetually annoyed with compliance issues or code violations.
- Dealing with tenants, who may not be paying their rent or may be constantly complaining.

A seller's exhaustion can translate into an opportunity for you. When a seller is willing to throw his or her hands in the air and give up is the time when you to come in with your optimism and buy the property at a discount. When frustrated, property owners don't realize the value of what they have and they will price their property at a fire-sale price just to unload it. That's when you come in with your fresh viewpoint on the value of the property. In many cases, the problems that the previous owner had are not anything that will impact your life in a negative way.

I recently heard about a twelve-unit townhouse development in one of Chicago's western suburbs. I knew this to be a premium area, and I thought the price on the project was very reasonable. The seller had owned it for quite some time, but had hired a property manager who didn't take care of the property very well; he wasn't collecting rents from tenants and had aggravated the city to the point where it frequently cited the property for building code violations. Even though the owner had owned the property for the last two decades, he was just frustrated and wanted to sell this real estate for a price lower than I thought it was worth. The seller simply didn't have the same vision of the property that I did. I looked ten years into the future and saw that this property would keep increasing in value; he saw only his own frustration. As a result, I had the opportunity to buy the property at a good price. I understood the obstacles that needed to be overcome, and I was looking to reap the rewards of his frustration.

Understanding the Perception of Property Values

Perception is extremely subjective: You may, for example, have a friend who enjoys a restaurant that you absolutely can't stand. The same subjective view plays into the perception of property values, too. One person may perceive that a property is worth very little; another person may view the property as quite valuable.

Sometimes a seller's perceived value of property is less than your perception of the property's value. In nearly every deal I've made, the seller thought he or she had gotten the better deal and was satisfied with the selling price. Thus, in every case, the seller's perception of value was different from mine and that has let me have some great opportunities.

Here's an example. About ten years ago, the owner of an auto body shop passed away, leaving his property to his children. The shop was located in a 50-by-120-foot garage located near a residential area that was getting popular. At the time I was approached to acquire this building, it was lined up next to two similar garages; in fact, this was auto mechanics row.

I felt that this area was going to be a boom area, so I decided to purchase the garage. However, I didn't want to carry the property (I wanted to flip it right away), so I stated in the contract that I needed six months to do an environmental audit to see whether the land had any pollution problems. During this period, the seller gave me permission to place a sign on the property that said "For Sale or Lease." (This just goes to show you that it pays to ask!) Just before the six months ended, I received a call from a Realtor who had a restaurant owner as a client. They both felt as I did that this neighborhood was a superb candidate for redevelopment. (Often, the first sign of rising real estate prices is when trendy restaurants open in an iffy neighborhood.) I had an asking price that was strong, so I accepted. Today, the neighboring garage buildings have been torn down for condominiums, townhouses are everywhere, the restaurant is thriving, and real estate prices are sky high.

The moral of this story? The owners perceived this property as a garage with little value. I saw it as much more than an old garage building and was able to make money on the deal.

Location, Location, Location

Yes, we all know that the same house that sells for $100,000 in a depressed area may be worth $1 million in a nice shorefront location. But there are many elements of a property's location and neighborhood that affect its value. Carefully examine all aspects of every property before you make a purchase. Here are the most relevant things to pay attention to when you consider purchasing a property:

- *Future neighborhood development.* Are there serious plans on anyone's drawing board that could affect your property?
- *Population of the area.* Is it growing, dwindling, or stable?
- *Potential for disaster.* Is the property located in an active flood plain, a tornado area, or an earthquake zone?
- *Zoning.* If you're looking at a commercial property or the possibility of converting a single-family residence to a multiunit, what are the current zoning regulations? Can you get the zoning changed if you want? Be sure to actually check the current zoning map for the area and call the alderman or councilman for the area to verify the zoning as well.
- *Traffic patterns.* Are nearby roads sufficient for their current traffic load? What changes may occur in the future?
- *Utilities.* Are they in place? Will you have to pay extra to get them in?
- *Schools.* If you're looking at a residential property, are there schools nearby? How good are they?

- *Recreation.* If you're looking at property for residential use, how attractive are the recreational opportunities in the area?
- *Safety.* How available are police, fire, and other services? What are the most recent crime statistics for the city or area?
- *Sanitation.* What are the provisions for sewerage and trash disposal? Is service provided by the town or city, or by private contractors?
- *Parking.* Is there sufficient room for parking on the property and in nearby streets?
- *Public transportation.* How close are the nearest bus stops or train stations?

Using Appraisals

Placing a value on real estate isn't scientific. It is based on subjectivity, perceptions, and the value of comparable pieces of property. However, no two pieces of real estate are identical, so how can an appraiser (a person who establishes the value of homes), accurately identify the value of property?

Although not exact, appraisers use four methods to value real estate:

- *Comparative square-foot method.* This technique estimates what builders are charging per square foot to build homes, and multiplies that amount by the number of square feet in the house.
- *Cost method.* Similar to comparative square-foot method, this method actually maps out what the land, construction materials, labor, and fixtures would cost if you were to build an identical house next door.
- *Comparable property method.* This method looks at property of similar size and in similar condition that has sold recently in the same or similar neighborhoods. With this

approach, the appraiser can estimate a value for your home based on how comparable homes have sold in the past.

- *Income approach*. This is a way of appraising property based on the assumption that it can earn income, as with a rental property.

I have found an amazing trend in appraisals: Appraisals almost always come in dollar for dollar where you would like them to come in. How does that happen? You may think that an appraisal would often come in higher or lower than your contract price. But the appraisal industry works like this: When an appraiser sees the real estate contract and observes what price you are paying for the property, he or she tries every method to come up with that specific value, because the mortgage lender, the seller, and the buyer will all be happy with that appraisal. In addition, I've seen less scrupulous appraisers appraise the property higher or lower than they should based on what the needs of the buyer or seller are. Is an appraisal needed for a tax assessment? Then it comes in low. Is it needed for a refinance? Then it comes in high. While this isn't usual, it does sometimes happen. What this means to you is appraisals are subjective; they can be based on many factors, but when all is said and done, they are subject to interpretation.

Keep in mind that some sellers obtain appraisals before they sell and will use them as a selling point. For example, a person may show you an appraisal for $200,000 but have an asking price of only $150,000. When this happens, warning bells should go off in your head. After all, why would somebody knowingly lose $50,000 on the sale of a property? Chances are this seller has obtained an appraisal at a higher value than what the property is worth. (By the way, in some areas, this is a criminal act that is punishable with fines or jail time!)

Alternatively, you may find yourself in a situation in which the appraisal comes in too low for you to get your financing. In this case, you need to go to bat for yourself and get the appraisal corrected, pointing out areas that were missed or incorrectly appraised. You can also hire your own appraiser to get a second opinion.

Knowing When Your Timing Is Right

You'll develop a sixth sense for when your timing is right. Just like you've known that anything else in your life was a good decision, you'll know when a piece of property is right, too. Go with your gut, as long as you follow the guidelines throughout this book for lining up your financing, working with an attorney, and finding good deals.

The most important reason to not purchase property that you plan to flip is that the price of a property you're considering buying is too high. Most potential real estate flips are in properties that are lower in price than they're worth. If a seller asks for a price that's too high (therefore making it impossible to make money on the flip), walk away from the deal and let the property go. Sometime in the future, that seller may reduce the price to a point where your buying it makes sense, but if not, start looking for other buying opportunities (see Chapter 6 for more details on identifying the best flipping opportunities).

If a potential deal is a good one, then it's worth taking the time to investigate it thoroughly. Time is one of the best investments you'll ever make in any real estate flip. Haste, on the other hand, can lead to many problems that you won't be aware of until it is too late. When considering a real estate purchase, slow down, take a deep breath, and follow these rules:

- Don't buy any property if something doesn't feel right about it or about the person you are buying it from. Trust your instincts.

- Don't buy if the salesperson is too pushy. If he or she is in such a hurry, it may mean that there are problems the salesperson is worried you will uncover, given a little more time.
- Don't buy a property that needs too much work. Keep looking for a property that is less likely to bring you stress and take up all of your time.
- Don't make overly optimistic projections of the income the property could bring you during a holding period.
- Most important, don't proceed before thoroughly researching the true value of the property and what you might be able to sell it for.

Chapter 8

How to Buy Real Estate

You begin flipping real estate by buying real estate, and this chapter shows you how to do it right. You find out how to make an offer, react to a counteroffer, and close the sale. Read this chapter, get your checkbook ready, and begin buying properties!

Making an Offer

Your first step in buying real estate is making an offer to purchase the property. This initial step involves filling out and signing a contract (keeping in mind that the seller will likely make a counteroffer) and putting down earnest money.

Using a contract

You need a contract to buy a property. If you're working with a Realtor, he or she will have a contract from the local real estate board. Otherwise, you can obtain a copy of the local real estate contract used in your area from a local title company or an attorney. If you use a generic form, be sure all of the fine print applies to the laws in your area by checking it first with a Realtor or attorney.

A contract must be in writing to be valid. Samuel Goldwyn, the movie producer, often said that "a verbal contract isn't worth the paper it's written on." If you try to base a deal on a handshake, you, too, will soon discover that a deal isn't a deal until you have a signature on a piece of paper, and sometimes not even until after that, when the ink is dry and the check is deposited.

To buy real estate, you submit a written contract offer to the seller. In the contract, you indicate the following:

- The price you're willing to pay for the real estate
- What's included in the sale (appliances and anything else not nailed down)
- The amount of earnest money you'll put down (see "Putting down earnest money" later in this chapter) and where the earnest money will be deposited
- How much time the seller has to think about and accept or decline the offer
- Whether the sale is contingent on your getting a mortgage and the amount of time you have to apply for that mortgage
- Whether you'll have an inspection done and in what time frame
- When you'll close the deal
- When you'll take possession (at the closing or several days or weeks afterward?)
- Which closing costs the buyer will pay; which closing costs the seller will pay
- Who's responsible for upcoming property taxes
- How much time you have for your attorney to review the contract (if any)

All these terms are important, yet depending on your deal, you may want to waive one or two of these items to sway the seller in your direction. Or, in reality, you just may not require all the contingencies. If you know you have the money to close the deal (say, in the form of a second mortgage, a credit line, or your own cash), you don't necessarily need to have a mortgage contingency in your contract. By eliminating a mortgage contingency, you appear to be making a cash deal, which is always appealing to a seller. In fact, with almost all properties I acquire, I eliminate the mortgage contingency from the contract. I have the credit lined up so that the seller is enthused about me as a buyer.

Expecting a counteroffer

When making an offer to buy real estate, keep in mind that the seller will nearly always make a higher counteroffer. In only rare cases does a seller simply accept your offer without making a counteroffer. Think of this as a game—the offer-counteroffer game—and this game always includes "gimmes": what you're willing to give away in order to make the seller feel that he or she is getting a good deal. Two tips for playing the game:

- Offer a lower price than you're willing to pay so that the seller can counteroffer a higher price.
- Ask for a longer inspection period than you need so that the seller can counteroffer with a shorter period.

For some reason, the sale of real estate (and automobiles, too, by the way) brings out the haggling mentality in everyone. People want to bargain back and forth. If you try to eliminate this custom, one party will feel taken advantage of. So make the deal as important as the real estate itself so that the seller has that warm fuzzy feeling in a deal. In the end, you win by profiting.

Putting down earnest money

With your offer, give the seller a check as earnest money, usually 10 percent or less of the price to acquire the property. The check is made payable to a third-party escrow agent, a Realtor, a title company, or an attorney, but usually not the seller. If the seller can't deliver the property to you, you don't want the seller to cash the check, making you worry about the return of your earnest money. Make sure your contract includes language that says exactly what will happen to the earnest money if the seller doesn't accept your offer or if the seller can't sell you the property for any reason. As long as you don't pull out of the agreement just because you changed your mind, you should have the earnest money returned to you.

Getting Your Offer Accepted or Reviewing a Counteroffer

One simple way to get your offer accepted is to offer the seller the price he or she is asking. Occasionally, the seller may figure that he's asking too little and want more, but basically if you give the seller what he asks for, you'll make a deal.

Sometimes, you find that the seller believes the value of the property is less than the market value as you see it. In late 1998, someone flipped me a property. (Yes, I buy property that I know was flipped if I still see value in it.) The seller from whom I acquired the property bought it at a discount and was able to resell to me at a discount. My intent was not to flip the property again, but to convert the building to condominiums that, just three years later, won an award from the Chicago Association of Realtors. But first came the offer-counteroffer game.

The neighbor to this property was an elderly woman in the restaurant business. This woman and her husband bought the six-unit building next door to mine. They found the property in the 1960s, when prices were much lower and the neighborhood wasn't nearly as popular. This couple first lived in the building and then bought a home in the suburbs and kept the property as a rental. The building itself was not on a lot size that you would expect a six-unit, center-entrance building to be built on (50 feet), but instead sat on 33.5 feet, which made all of the apartments long and narrow, like railroad cars. The property had also fallen into disrepair; the bricks had lost mortar, windows were broken, and so on. The owner, now a widow, was a sharp woman who spent money only when the city hit her with violations. She had no mortgage because the building was paid off years before. Periodically, she visited the property to collect rent.

One day she noticed the renovation work I was doing on my property next door, and she approached me to see if I wanted to buy hers. She would say, "Mr. Weiss, you should buy my building. I am old, and I can't take care of the property. The city is after me, and the tenants don't pay. You should do to my property what you did to yours. You are so wise and so generous; can you help me and buy my property?"

I, of course, was being set up, but I knew this was a developing area and the property had value, so the offer-counteroffer game began. She would invite me into the property, we would sit down, and she would ask me what I wanted to pay her for the building. Then I would ask how much she wanted. She wouldn't answer, and I would sit silently. We both knew that whoever spoke first would lose. (Ever try to sit silently with another person? Usually, someone wants to burst. I am well practiced at this, so I can sit forever!) Finally, she had to throw a number out, and I agreed to pay it. The following day, she informed me it was too low, and wouldn't you know it, someone just came along and offered her $10,000 more. Then the game went something like this:

> *Mrs. Seller:* "You know, Mr. Weiss, that I can't manage the property, and the city is all over me. I am sick, and I can't collect rent. You are young, energetic,

and handsome (I may be exaggerating a bit there!), and you should buy my building and make good money. I want $450,000."

Weiss: "I understand, Mrs. Seller, that you want $450,000 for your building. Because you told me I was handsome, I agree to pay you $450,000. I have a contract here. Let's sign it. I have my check-book, too, so I can make out an earnest money check to the title company."

Mrs. Seller: "Well, let me think about it. I will talk to my son and call you tomorrow."

Then, the following day, I got a phone call:

Mrs. Seller: "You know, I have a neighbor who has decided he's going to pay me $455,000."

Weiss: "Well, Mrs. Seller, I know that I am handsome and all that, and that you can't handle the property any longer. But it's 9:00 A.M. on a Monday morning, and I saw you last evening at 7:00 P.M. Did you get a call in the middle of the night from someone else out of the blue or in your dream? Well, you drive a hard bargain, but because you flatter me, I'll pay you $455,000. I would like to come right over with a contract and a check and get things rolling. When can we meet today?"

Mrs. Seller: "Let me think about it. I need to go to the doctor now, and then I need to talk to my attorney; I'll call you back."

Then, the next day:

Mrs. Seller: "You know, Mr. Weiss; I think I have an offer for $460,000. Would you pay me $460,000?"

Weiss: "Are you willing to sign a contract with me today?"

Mrs. Seller: "Well, yes."

Weiss: "Yes, Mrs. Seller, I'll pay you $460,000. I would like to come right over with a contract and a check and get things rolling. When can we meet today?"

Mrs. Seller: "You know, Mr. Weiss, I just remembered I have to work today. I'll call you tomorrow."

This continued on and on. Finally, she agreed on a price to sell me the building—$480,000. It took three months, but I thought she had finally reached her limit. I knew no one else was on the sidelines waiting to make an offer, but I also knew that I could flip it for $550,000, so I was still ahead.

I had my attorney draft a contract for me. Mrs. Seller came to my office, which was a big move toward making the deal. I presented her with a contract to sign with all the terms previously agreed upon. She wouldn't sign it. She wanted her attorney to approve the contract first. Two days later, her attorney called mine with three or four minor changes in the legal language. After the lawyer reviewed those changes, he then said to my attorney, "You know, she now wants $20,000 more in price."

My attorney called to inform me of the changes, not knowing the rigmarole I had gone through already. So, I informed my attorney to inform the seller that I was not interested at all. She could keep the building. I knew I had to stop negotiations. I was done. I knew that she had no one else to sell the property to, and I knew she would come back to me, but I didn't know when.

Then, several years later, in March 2002, I received a call from her: "Mr. Weiss, this is Mrs. Seller. I will sell the property for $550,000." Although that seemed like a lot more, by that time, I knew I could resell for almost $700,000. I called my secretary and told her to call the seller and have her attorney draft a contract and then forward a signed sales contract for me to accept. When I returned to my office, it was waiting. I signed it. She thought she had me, and she was thrilled. She could have gotten more, but she did not want to pay a fee. And she got $100,000 more from me than she would have if we had closed with the initial offer. The day after the closing, I posted a "For Sale" sign on the property. Ten days later, I sold the building for $667,000, through a Realtor, to a developer who planned to convert the property to condos. So, I made money, too, and the developer is selling the six units for $230,000 each, so he will gross $1,380,000 in the end.

So my advice for the offer-counteroffer game is this: Be patient, stick to your guns, and when the counteroffering gets out of control, stop.

Getting an Inspection

In most real estate contracts you will have a contingency for an inspection. When you are flipping property, setting an inspection contingency can be used for reasons other than the normal expectation of simply inspecting the property and looking for defects. Of course you will inspect the property for defects, but the contingency can also be used as a delaying tactic, giving you a longer time to try to resell the property before you close, or as a negotiating tool to get a better price after you list the defects you or your inspector has found. I suggest you begin with ten working days for the inspection of residential properties. You can always extend that date later.

In the early stages of looking for a property to flip, it is important to get the names of inspectors and check their references as well. Often your Realtor can be an excellent resource.

The critical inspection is the environmental audit that looks for underground storage tanks or soil pollution from chemical disposal on the premises or in drains. The environmental inspection or audit is a negotiating point that is very important in commercial flips because you just don't know what's under the property and what might lead to an expensive cleanup for you in the future. Also, in a practical sense, your buyer will most likely require you to provide him or her with a clean bill of health in the form of a phase-one environmental audit (an overview of the environmental history of the property and a list of potential problems for follow-up if any are required), because the buyer will probably need financing, and the lender will most likely require one.

Your environmental audit inspection will take longer than ten days. Check with an environmental company before you write up a paragraph for that contingency because, depending on how active your market is, you will need to take thirty to sixty days for the environmental inspection. During this time you can require access to the property and begin your preselling of the property to save yourself some time.

What inspectors do

Now let's talk about how inspections work. You certainly want to find a good property inspector, someone who is not going to be a deal breaker. You need to interview inspectors to prepare them for what you are looking for in the inspection report and what your intent is in flipping the property. If you have a Realtor, find someone your Realtor has worked with successfully. The inspector should be someone who can set you on the path with his or her knowledge and guidance; after working with the inspector, you should be able to better understand what needs to be completed or is defective, and what is in working order or needs to be in working order when you acquire the property.

Establish the inspector's fee ahead of time; this usually runs in the $200 to $300 range. This is money well spent, because a couple of hundred dollars spent now can save you from buying a property that will cost you thousands and thousands of dollars down the road. Even after you feel that you have become experienced in evaluating properties, continue to hire inspectors. You still may overlook something, and it is good to have a second opinion from an experienced professional who most likely has seen just about everything before.

Everyone comes to the table with their own subjective set of standards, but for the most part, if you get the property you want and can flip it and make money, you have won! Let's say that you are making an offer on a residential property, for example. It's a fixer-upper, and you already know you are going to replace the kitchen. In your offer you have taken into consideration the cost of repairs and renovation for that kitchen, so if your home inspector points out that you need a new kitchen, you shouldn't look at that as a fear factor in the deal. Ask your inspector to look for the stuff you can't and don't see. You shouldn't try to renegotiate the items that you already know you have negotiated in your price. This might kill the deal.

Does what I'm saying make sense? Well, in some cases people try to renegotiate and to take advantage of situations that they know they have already addressed in the price. Sometimes people try to use the home inspection contingency to hold the seller hostage, even though by putting too much pressure on the seller after receiving the home inspection report you may actually kill your deal. It's important to deal with your Realtor and talk with him or her about various things that come up. But what I've found with home inspectors is that some of them point out to you normal and conventional things, but depict them in a catastrophic way. That's where you need to gain enough experience to know that the burned-out light bulb is not an electrical problem throughout the building. There are also very good home inspectors who present in an accurate and realistic way those things that are issues and nonissues related to repairing and maintaining your unit.

If you are buying a vintage building and there are areas of the property that settled a hundred years ago, you need to know that this is really a nonissue and doesn't need your attention, because the building has been otherwise sound for an entire century. But for the most part an inspector will show you items that you may not know to look for. Sometimes, simply sticking a pencil in a small hole behind the wall will indicate there are termites in the building that have created a spongy softness to the wood and thus you may need to replace certain items that you weren't aware of. Sticking a coin under a tile may let you know that you need to replace tile on a bathroom wall. By walking into a closet and lifting the wall-to-wall carpet in the corner, you might be surprised to find hardwood flooring, a definite bonus. A good inspector will let you know the lifetime of the heating unit that you have in the property. You might not have known that a brand-new water heater has been installed, or, on the other hand, that you have an old water heater that's rusting from the bottom and might cost you an additional $460 to replace, plus face the risk of flooding your neighbor's condominium apartment. Whatever the case may be, having a home inspection is important for you to know what you are buying, but also to let you know that you are buying a property that's not going to be running into excessive repair dollars once the deal has closed.

The environmental audit

A few decades ago, people became much more aware of our environment and sensitive to the problems related to it. This has affected real estate in a number of ways. My experience began twenty years ago when during an appraisal of an apartment building I was selling for a bank, the appraiser noted there was asbestos pipe wrap in the boiler room. Asbestos was used commonly before 1960 to insulate pipes in buildings with central heating systems. The lender would not approve the loan unless the asbestos was removed. This is a benign example of the extent of the audits that take place now. Many buildings were previously heated by oil, and they may have abandoned underground storage tanks that still have oil in them or have leaked oil at some time. Certainly many businesses have disposed of chemicals and chemical waste inappropriately. As a result, lenders have created a requirement specifying that, in most cases, properties have to be inspected for environmental compliance. Today the environmental issue that everyone is concerned about in residential real estate is mold. Mold from moisture that builds up over years and is a health problem, and the long and the short of this is that everything can be remedied by spending money. What you should do is require that the seller give you a clean phase one-environmental audit, and problems that are discovered in the audit should be remedied prior to closing. Most often your seller will not be aware of existing problems, or won't have the cash to clean up the property. To use this as an advantage, you can pay for the property cleanup from the proceeds of the sale at closing, or agree that you will pay for the cleanup prior to closing and lower the price, or require that your buyer do the cleanup at his or her own expense later, and just walk away with some more money.

You can, as mentioned earlier in this chapter, take the time provided for in the audit period and sell the real estate before closing. Time in flipping is important. Once you close you are paying interest and losing profit. Prior to closing, the expense of carrying the property is passed on to the seller and not to you.

Read the Fine Print

Before getting to the closing, make sure you know exactly what you are getting into. Read all documents carefully, preferably with your lawyer. Many people don't like to muddle through such documents. They give the papers a quick once-over, and they sign their lives away. Instead, you should go over every document page by page, paragraph by paragraph, line by line, and word by word. When making an investment, it is your responsibility to understand your rights and responsibilities for yourself.

You also need to be sure that you understand all the procedures outlined and terms used in any papers. Ask your lawyer to explain things to you, or look up any words you don't understand (many such terms can be found in the glossary in the back of this book). This is not the time to fake your way through a technical conversation.

Become familiar with your documents and what obligations they entail. If you don't know things such as your interest rate and whether it's fixed or adjustable, when payments are due, and your legal liabilities, you may end up losing that property to the company that loaned you the money to buy it.

Closing the Deal

A closing meeting is where the deed is transferred from owner to buyer. The closing may be held at a title company, or a title officer may come to a real estate office, or more than likely it's held at an attorney's office. The money and documents are usually put into escrow, which simply means that a third party, the title company, inspects all documents and dollars, makes sure that everything is in order, and distributes these to the appropriate party. Factors to be checked include: that the seller actually owns the property you are buying, that your check is good and not going to bounce, that the survey is accurate (and that the railroad does not have permission to run that line through your front yard!), and that basically everything is in order. You must have a closing through a title company because it provides insurance to you in case it makes a mistake on verifying the title and other documents. I know of many cases where money changed hands, but the title officer was not watching the closing documents that changed hands and the buyer was sold a bill of goods, but not the property. The insurance from the title company provided financial reward to make the buyer whole.

Arranging the financing

To close any real estate deal, you need money. Even if you're going to quickly flip the property to someone else, you still need money. (See Chapter 4 for advice on lining up your financing.) Planning to sell the property immediately after buying it (called a dual closing where you buy and sell at the same time) can get a little tricky; in fact, I have known of situations in which a buyer planned to do two closings, but couldn't find a buyer before the closing. (See the next section in this chapter for more on managing a dual closing.) The bottom line is, before you make an offer, have your financing in place, no matter how confident you are that you can quickly line up a buyer for that property. You just never know.

In 1996, two young men came to see me. They were Realtors who found out about a foreclosure taking place the following month. They knew the property had value and they intended to contact the owner, give him a little money, and make a profit flipping his property. They persuaded the owner to sign a contract and convinced him that they could close prior to the foreclosure, so that he wouldn't lose the property, but instead could pay his mortgagee, take care of the real estate taxes he owed, and walk away with a little bit of money in the bank. They also paid him $10,000 cash up front so that he would be persuaded.

The problem was that these two buyers didn't have the capability to close. They were hoping to find a buyer so that they could arrange a dual closing, but they couldn't find one. They had the right idea, but they were running out of time and hadn't lined up their financing in advance. Had they backed out, they would have lost the opportunity and their $10,000 (the owner had already spent it). Fortunately for them, I got involved and saved the transaction, but those two real estate flippers came close to blowing a good deal and losing money because they hadn't made arrangements in advance.

Don't put yourself in that position. Before you make an offer, be sure you have the money to close the deal—credit lines, home equity lines, partners, or whatever else you need to secure your position. Even at a high interest rate, if the property is a good deal, having the financing in place will be worthwhile.

Planning a dual closing, simultaneous closings, or two separate closings

Many people buy property to flip; hold on to it for a week, a month, or even several years; and then sell it when they find a seller who's willing and able to pay a price that brings a profit. On the other hand, you may decide to try to sell the property the moment you buy it. The main advantage to going this route—a dual closing—is that you don't need as much cash on hand as you would need for a single closing. You can buy and sell at the same time, with your buyer coming to the closing with enough money to buy from you and pay off the party from whom you're buying the property. The disadvantage is that you need a buyer lined up at the same time you locate a piece of property.

A dual closing often makes the other seller and buyer feel as though they've been cheated, especially when your buyer realizes how much *less* you paid for the property, and the seller realizes how much *more* you're making on the resale. So, you may want to conduct a simultaneous closing, where each takes place in a separate room, with the title company providing two sets of title insurance and paying for two separate closings. (Be sure to check in advance whether the title company can orchestrate this type of transaction.) Here's how the simultaneous closing works: Your buyer arrives first and puts his or her money into an escrow account; then the title company transfers that money to your seller's escrow.

Arranging for simultaneous closings costs you a bit more money because of additional closing fees related to the sale, but if you conduct a dual closing, you run the risk of making both other parties feel uncomfortable and, potentially, of either one backing out of the deal or making their own deal together. They'd lose some money in closing costs if they walked away from your deal, but they could make that up with a higher profit for the seller and a lower buying cost for the buyer. As a result, I've never conducted a flip with my buyer and seller in the same room. I've either had simultaneous closings at the same title company or arranged for two totally separate closings, either hours or days apart. In separate closings, you buy and take control of the property and sell it some other day.

Chapter 9

Honing Your Negotiating Skills

You need to be able to negotiate in order to flip real estate. This chapter will help you to hone your negotiating skills so that you can make the best deals as you flip properties.

Getting to the Decision Maker

Before you begin negotiating, you need to find out who will decide whether to buy or sell a piece of property—in other words, you need to get to the decision maker. You may, for example, meet with a husband, but the wife is really the one who makes the decisions. Sometimes a partner that you never meet or a financial advisor who is somewhere out in the wings is the real decision maker. It may be a person who sits in a meeting with nothing to say and is simply watching and observing while the others are actively partic-ipating, or it may be someone who you never actually see. In a corporate setting, the decision maker may be an officer of the corporation who has been assigned to dispose of or acquire a piece of property. On the other hand, the officer of the corporation may have to go before a board of directors before any decision can be reached.

You need to get to the decision maker in order to be sure that the person you're dealing with can't put the burden of making a decision on someone else. So, if the person from whom you're buying property tells you that he or she can't make a decision before talking to his or her partner, you're on hold while they take their time.

To get to the decision maker, you need to do a bit of investigative work. Ask some of the following to help you assess the situation so that you know with whom to negotiate:

- Why do you want to sell now?
- How long have you thought about selling?
- Do you have another place to live?
- Do you have any partners?
- Have you discussed selling the property with your partners?
- Do your partners want to sell now?
- How long have you owned the property?
- How many units comprise the property?
- What are the real estate taxes?
- What is your mortgage balance?
- Who pays the expenses (heating, electric, real estate taxes, insurance, water, scavenger, and other maintenance costs)?
- Is the property tenant-heated (does the landlord pay the heat or does each tenant pay for that unit's heat)?
- Do you have a management company to manage the property?
- Have you had a recent appraisal of the property?
- What do you feel the property is worth?
- How did you arrive at that value?

Your purpose for asking questions is simple: You need to make sure you're talking to a prospective seller, and you need to make sure the seller is ready to sell at a fair price. If you're ready to make a deal, but the seller isn't, you'll waste your time. Of all the questions just listed two are most important: Why do you want to sell now? Do you have any partners?

Why do you want to sell now?

This is your most important question, and you need to get a good, substantive answer that makes sense to you, such as: We're getting divorced, we need the liquidity, my father just died and we don't want to own the real estate, we owe the bank a lot of money and we have to pay it off, when the property was acquired initially we knew we would hold it for eight years and it would pay for our son's college education, and so on. If the response is something more along the lines of, "I really don't want to sell now," keep this person on your radar and keep checking back—you may eventually find a time when that person will want to sell.

Do you have any partners?

Years ago, I met with two adult children who wanted to sell their parents' house. They approached me to acquire the property, and I was rather anxious to do so. I put a contract on the property and it was accepted. Shortly thereafter, when I was looking to flip the property, I took a risk and put an ad in the paper and received a call from someone who appeared to be an interested third party. However, when I described the property and gave the address, the person told me I would never be able to buy that building. I was surprised because I had a signed contract and an earnest-money check that had been cashed. But the person on the phone was the husband of the third sibling of the sellers, and the property couldn't be sold unless all three siblings agreed to sell it. The other two siblings had never told me about the third one, and, although they had gotten me excited and enthusiastic about buying the property, I forgot to ask the critical question, "Do you have any partners?" To avoid a lawsuit, the two who had signed the contract paid me for my time and effort, but I had wasted a great deal of time for nothing.

Making the Seller Happy

You make a seller happy by meeting his or her needs. That may include one or all of the following:

- Meeting (or exceeding) the asking price that is acceptably close enough
- Making the seller feel as though he or she got a great deal or got away with something
- Closing by a certain day (for example, allowing the seller to get into another house at that same time, to pay off a property tax debt, to have cash to invest in a business, and so on)
- Selling to someone the seller likes
- Ensuring that the deal will go through (for example, agreeing not to get a mortgage or have an inspection done)
- Buying the property at a later date (say, in one year), while paying a little cash now

Try to think in terms of meeting the seller's needs as you go through your negotiations. If you're the only one who gets anything good out of the deal, you haven't made the seller happy, and you likely won't end up owning—and then flipping—the property. Give a little, and you'll both be happy.

Developing Your Listening Skills

One of the best traits to develop, no matter what business you're in, is the ability to listen. There's a significant difference between *hearing* and *listening*. When you really listen, you understand the problem, situation, or opportunity that someone is presenting to you. Listening means understanding, even when you don't agree with the point of view of the person you're speaking with. When you can really listen, you can be honest and fair because you can work on the heart of the situation, not what you think you might have heard. You will often find, after truly listening, that what seemed like big obstacles and disagreements at first are really not that significant at all.

Sometimes things are just as they seem to be; yet at other times, we can understand what people are actually telling us only by taking a step back and listening to the whole story. Often I will have conversations with people who talk about their property with pride, and discuss their property in ways that make me know, regardless of how they have responded to my letter or call or initial contact, they never want to sell their property! How do I know this? I *listen* carefully to what people tell me and read past the words into their emotions and body language. A lot of what I "hear" I actually see in the people I talk to. I try to listen to an inner voice interpreting the message as it is conveyed by someone using all their communication tools.

Finding out that the seller really doesn't want to sell is one thing, but finding out that the seller is hiding something is another important reason to learn to listen. You may find yourself talking to a seller who is telling you how great things are and how much he or she really wants to keep the real estate, but in reality the seller absolutely cannot! This is when you realize that the weak link in the seller's chain creates an opportunity for you to acquire the property.

It is not unusual for me to ask a prospective seller if he or she is really interested in selling a particular building and then get a positive description about the property in response. I certainly feel positive about the real estate as well—otherwise I wouldn't be considering acquiring the property. But as the conversation continues I sometimes come to realize through various messages and signals that, although I am sitting in the seller's office having a cup of coffee together under the guise of making a deal at some point, the seller really has no intention of selling.

I developed this listening skill many years ago when I was in the commercial real estate field looking for listings. I would make cold calls to people and find that many people, especially senior citizens, would invite me over to their home or their office to talk about selling their real estate. I'd learn they were receiving income, they had no real need to sell the property, but as a young rookie in the field I was always tempted by the invitation to come and talk about their property. I didn't realize at first that, while I was thinking these people were planning to sign a listing agreement with me and I would be earning a big fat commission, basically they just needed someone to spend the afternoon with. Since I'm a quick study, I discovered this in no time at all, but I still see people spending hours with nonsellers who I can easily identify will never be sellers.

Early in 2003, a seller called me after having received my letter telling him that I was interested in buying property. We set a date to inspect his fifteen-unit property on a cold rainy day. I loved the property. It was just what I was looking for. We toured the building and he showed me all the work he had done over the years and he told me with great pride all of his history with the property. The more he showed me the more excited I got about this deal. But I soon found myself yawning. This was a sign to me, I realized, that he was not a seller. I was bored. I wanted to talk the deal, while he wanted to talk about chain-link storage lockers. He just wanted to show off the property. I was probably just one of many interested parties he called and spent time with sharing his life experiences in property management and restoration. Really, I was not interested in his tales; I just wanted the property. This man was not a seller, even though initially he answered my questions appropriately. I'm still in touch with him, but he certainly is not ready now. But I do want to be there when he is ready.

Using the Power of Silence

You may wonder how silence helps you negotiate, but it really can work wonders. Being silent—that is, taking your time to answer when on the phone or in a meeting, or taking the time to respond to an offer or other piece of information—creates a certain amount of anxiety for the other party, especially if he or she is anxious to make a deal.

When someone waits for an answer from you, he or she usually believes you're not interested, and so begins to give away more: The seller may lower the price, reduce the commission, change the time line, agree to inspection and/or mortgage clauses that weren't on the table at the beginning, and so on. Generally, the more standoffish you are, the more aggressive the other party becomes in finding a way to make the deal happen. It's just the result of nervous butterflies for the other party, but it's a tremendous negotiating tool.

I've talked to people who want to buy or sell real estate and have to make a deal within a certain time frame to satisfy certain needs—of course, this makes them sitting ducks for a good negotiator whose silence can make them squirm. I'm currently dealing with people who want to buy a shopping center in a wonderful location on Chicago's north side, and need to sell an apartment building at the same time to cover the financing. I'm not exactly sure what their attachment is to the shopping center (I see many other viable alternatives for investing in the marketplace), but I get calls from this partnership very frequently. They're getting nervous. I want to buy this apartment building, but the longer I stay silent, the more likely they are to lose the opportunity to buy this large shopping center. You want to develop the ability to know when someone is on a hot seat and when being silent in a negotiation can work in your favor.

Make a Reasonable Offer

When it comes to a fair price for a property, the rule of thumb is: There is no rule of thumb—every property is different, even from others on the same block. If a property is offered at a reasonable $400,000, common sense tells you not to offer an unreasonable $200,000. Some people start negotiating by offering half of the stated purchase price, which is a clear sign that they are trying to play the win/lose game.

Many buyers begin by offering 10 to 15 percent below the stated price. That's usually okay, but don't consider the figure a rule of thumb applicable in all situations. *Make a respectable offer that makes good economic sense for all parties.* Generally, you'll receive a counteroffer. That's all part of the negotiating process. If a counteroffer doesn't come in, you can always go back with a slightly higher offer yourself.

Be Patient

Good things come to those who wait. The other day I was buying some office supplies, and whatever I was buying led the checkout clerk to ascertain that I am in the real estate business. He initiated a conversation with me, telling me that he lives in a building that he wants to buy: He is interested in buying real estate and once worked for a mortgage broker, so he's familiar with interest rates and the cost of borrowing money. He believed that everything would fall into place if he could just buy the building he lives in. After hearing his story about how interested and how aggressive he was, I asked him, "Is your seller ready to sell?" and he answered, "No."

So I asked him, "Why are you getting so excited if you have no control over the deal?" He wasn't sure. I asked, "What gives you the idea that your seller wants to sell?" He indicated to me that he understood that the owner's wife didn't like living in the property and wanted to move out of state. I said, "Well if that's the decision maker in this transaction, persuade the owner's wife that she lives in a terrible place and should move back to the East Coast with her husband. You have to be patient."

The bottom line is that he was telling me all about the deal he was going to make when he really had no control over the deal, didn't have a motivated seller, and was living in a fantasy about buying a particular property. He wasn't being patient; he was jumping the gun. Instead, he needed to plant seeds, cultivate and water them, and provide plenty of sunshine.

If you have a property that you're excited about but isn't available at the moment, be sure you reinforce to the property owners that you want to buy their property and that you think it's a good deal. But then you just have to be patient. I've seen people push a property owner to sell his or her property when the owner has no intention of selling. The push continues until the property owner never wants to deal with the buyer again. The owner is so upset and irritated by the constant annoyance that he or she sells to someone else who was able to develop a little more mature, less anxiety-producing relationship. Silence can be golden.

Negotiation Tips

How to negotiate a contract is something you can really only learn over time and with direct experience. Here are three more tips that can give you an edge in your first negotiations:

1. *Build an edge for yourself.* Try to conduct sessions on your own turf, in your office or office complex, or, if at all possible, insist on a neutral site.
2. *When negotiations stall, briefly walk out.* To avoid appearing rude, you have to do this correctly. Suggest a break and then walk out of the room before anyone can disagree. When you feel it's the right time or when you've been asked to return, be prepared with a new idea or a new slant to add to the negotiations.
3. *Give concessions slowly and one at a time.* It's important for the other party to feel that he or she has worked for each "gimme" that you give up.

Part Four

Holding and Selling

Chapter 10

Holding Properties to Increase Value

R eal estate—unlike some purchases such as cars or clothing—appreciates in value. This means that it gains value over time. Some real estate appreciates a great deal because the location or some other feature makes a lot of people want to buy it. Other times, real estate actually depreciates (loses value), because the price the buyer paid for it was too high, and no one wants to pay that amount again.

For the most part, however, if you buy real estate and hold on to it, it will gain in value. The trick is knowing how long to hold it. Hold it for too short a period of time, and you may miss out on reaping the benefits of greater appreciation in value. Hold it for too long, and you risk having your money tied up in property that's not appreciating in value as well as some other property might.

This chapter will help you understand how long you should hold on to property that you've purchased.

How Long Is Long Enough?

You are reading this book because you want to make money, but you should forget about trying to find a true get-rich-quick scheme. In my experience, all the people I have observed getting rich quickly have also been successful at losing it quickly. Although buying and selling real estate is not about getting rich quickly, you don't have to hold on to it forever to make a profit. How long is long enough? It depends on how much money you want to make and how the real estate market is going to react to your property.

An important factor to take into consideration when holding properties is that not all properties sell as quickly as you might like. About a year and a half ago, I acquired two buildings I wanted to flip, so I put both on the market at the same time. The first one sold within five months of my acquiring it. Considering that part of that period fell between Thanksgiving and Christmas (when almost no one buys real estate), five months wasn't too long to hold a property. After eighteen months, the second building still has not sold. But, because I bought it at the right price, I know that my margin is strong enough to withstand a longer wait. When I flip the second building, I'll walk away with a good profit, even though my holding period was longer for this property than it was for the first.

It's difficult to know how long things will be in your portfolio before they sell. Anyone with a good idea of how real estate works understands that sometimes there are no customers in a market. You can lower a price to a point of desperation and still have no one responding to your ads and acquiring the property.

Another consideration when deciding how long to hold a property is what profit margins you are looking for, and how quickly you need to achieve them. Some friends and colleagues of mine who flip real estate are happier with different ranges of profit than I am. Some are interested in a very quick volume of turnover, and some would rather hold properties so that they maximize their dollars.

I think it's crucial to be good at selling in any type of

market in order to make sure that the carrying costs of the real estate—the taxes, the insurance, and the interest rate—don't drag you down. At the same time, you have to be able to afford to carry your property long enough to make a profit. You need to decide for yourself what the best time line of flipping is for you, and you shouldn't worry about comparing the pace you flip properties at to that of anyone else.

Certainly everybody would like to see property sell fast. But when historical and economic events affect the economy, sometimes you'll find that things take a little longer. I've known people who've had rental property for a long enough period of time that the tenants are actually paying the mortgage and other expenses, and the seller has no money out of pocket at all. As a result, there is no pressure to sell during the holding period. In truth, the second property I am still trying to sell, which I mentioned earlier, has a tenant, and her rent offsets some of my expenses. There is also no debt on the property, so I'm not making any interest payments. My carrying cost is minimal at best.

Cash Flow and Appreciation

People buy rental property for the cash flow it will bring when held, or for the profit it will bring after being resold—or for both reasons. Cash flow (that is, income) is basically what's left over at the end of the month after you've paid your mortgage and other expenses. If you have no income left over, it may be the result of problems such as low rents, high expenses, or excessive vacancies. You will need to analyze the situation to see if you can change any elements to create a positive cash flow.

In some situations, even with all your best efforts, the cash flow will just be enough to cover the necessary payments (mortgage, taxes, utilities, maintenance, and repairs) on the property. This still may be all right, because your property isn't costing you anything during the time you own it. During the holding period, the property is usually appreciating in value, and you are therefore gaining capital. You may buy a property for $100,000, break even on the carrying costs, and in four years the property may be worth $130,000. This will give you an additional $30,000 to invest when you sell the property.

Knowing How Long Is Too Long

You've been holding a piece of property too long when any one of the following things occurs:

1. *You begin eating up your profit with interest and other carrying costs.* Carrying costs are the real dollars it takes to hold real estate—monthly interest, insurance, repairs and maintenance, municipal fees, points on the loan, advertising for tenants, utility bills, and other costs. Certainly, if your profit is being eaten away by interest or taxes, and you won't make a profit on the property, then it's time to sell.

2. *You just can't stand the maintenance and repairs anymore.* My own accountant bought a small building with the intention of either keeping it or, somewhere down the line, selling it and buying something else. But the management headaches, compliance with city codes, and other challenges that sometimes go along with owning real estate beat her up to the point where she just wanted to sell the property and get out.

3. *You are frustrated because you cannot find a good tenant—or any tenant at all.* We all think that we hang up a "For Rent" sign and tenants—good, honest tenants with good credit who pay the rent

on time—come. That situation is not always the case, however. I have run many credit reports only to discover that finding a qualified tenant to accept is more difficult and frustrating than it seems.

4. *You're tired of the many annoyances of managing a difficult property.* Perhaps you have gone to court to pay a citation one too many times because your trash container was overloaded.

5. *You find that, basically, the property is simply adding a lot of anxiety to your daily life.* Every time the phone rings, it's that same vocal tenant complaining about the leaky faucet. You thank the Lord for caller ID. You don't look forward to the mail coming, because you'll have to deal with complaining tenants. Or, even worse, one of your tenants got your cell phone number and published it on her Web site.

Before you buy property, be sure you know how long you can hold it before it starts to eat up your profit. And think about what will happen in an economic downturn. The first few years of the twenty-first century brought all sorts of economic headaches: The stock market crash, the crash of tech stocks, September 11th, airline layoffs, the corporate deceit of Enron, and the war in Iraq affected everyone in an economic sense. Many people who were just entering markets (whether stock markets, equity markets, or real estate markets) were blindsided because they didn't have a clear plan for selling their assets. Do your homework so that you know what the true cost of a property is going to be.

Creating Value Through Sweat Equity

To make money in real estate, you buy property, hold on to it for a certain period of time, and sell it for a higher price.

You can make money another way, however, and that is by sprucing up the property before you sell it. Sweat equity is another term for making improvements to your real estate: You sweat, and your share (equity) of the value of the house goes up. Improvements range from simple jobs like painting and decorating to major projects like installing a new bathroom or kitchen.

Improving bathrooms and kitchens is the best choice for increasing value to any property. People like large bathrooms that look clean and fresh, and modern kitchens with dishwashers, disposals, microwaves, attractive cabinets, and granite counters. You need to be careful, though, because you can easily overimprove a property and receive no return on your expenditures. A custom whirlpool in the deck, expensive wallpaper, opulent light fixtures, and skylights won't add the same value as simpler upgrades to kitchens and baths. And even in those rooms you need to spend time and money wisely. In this country, adding a bidet in the bathroom means nothing. Installing a marble shower stall and a reasonably priced whirlpool tub, on the other hand, does make a difference. Check with your local real estate agent for suggestions of what is most highly valued in your market. Not all of the same upgrades or improvements found in homes in Atlanta, Georgia, will be required or valued in Muskegon, Michigan, and vice versa.

Some repairs are necessary, of course. If the roof leaks, then while you are fixing everything else make absolutely certain that you repair the roof. Few people realize that a roof repair is really not catastrophic, but just another expense. But a problem with a roof is one thing that will scare potential buyers away.

When making improvements to a property, you should consider . . .

- Installing a modern kitchen with many cabinets, a disposal, dishwasher, and granite counters.

- Renovating a bathroom to include a whirlpool tub (though many people will never use it, they still like it), a new toilet, deep medicine cabinets, quiet fans, and as much light as possible.
- Tearing up the carpeting and refinishing any hardwood floors.
- In older homes with small rooms, opening the rooms to a different floor plan. People don't often use a formal dining room anymore, and many people prefer instead to have the large rooms called "great rooms" just off the kitchens.
- Keeping colors of paint and decorating trims neutral.
- Enlarging the garage if possible.

Here are some items that won't add much value and may in fact lose you money:

- Expensive carpeting or wallpaper
- Designer paint colors or drapes
- Expensive lighting fixtures
- Too much customization

Remember, everyone likes to add their own touches, and your best decorating efforts won't always be to someone else's taste. Make sure the property will be attractive and useful for a typical everyman or everywoman.

Getting Work Done

Some people hire contractors to do the work, but keep in mind that when you do that, you may not actually add to the value of the home: The amount you pay might just equal the additional amount that a buyer will be willing to pay.

For a major job, you almost certainly will have to hire a contractor (see Chapter 4 for more on finding and

evaluating contractors). When you are making major renovations to a property, make absolutely certain that you get
all necessary construction permits. Trying to get around this
requirement will only come back to hurt you. The few dollars you "save" will be nowhere near the amount of legal
fees and penalties you might receive for proceeding before
you receive a permit. Never hire a contractor who promises
to get the work done without a construction permit.

Rebuilding roofs or foundations and rewiring or
replumbing a structure does take time and money; there's
no way around it. Spend the money, get the permit, and do
it right. Getting the permit should be the responsibility of
the contractor, subcontractor, or general contractor, but
make sure you receive the original permit, currently
stamped and dated, for your files. But having the permit
doesn't guarantee that your contractor or subcontractor will
do the work according to code. For this reason, be sure to
pay a contractor only after you establish that the work was
done completely and in full compliance with the appropriate codes.

Going Condo

One interesting way to use contractors and still make a
profit is to turn rental properties into condominiums (see
more on this in Chapter 12). Typically, rental units aren't
kept in the best shape. They don't usually offer the better-
quality cabinets or appliances, the bathrooms may be small
and poorly designed, the heating system may not be
working property, and windows and walls may have been
damaged. If you buy, let's say, a fourteen-unit apartment
building and can pay a contractor to upgrade the kitchens
and baths, put in a new heating boiler, and repair the walls
and windows, the property will be much more attractive.
Even if you pay a contractor $40,000 per unit, if you bought

the building at $100,000 per unit and sell for $170,000 per condominium, you'll still make $420,000 in profit! As long as you can make the place look like a place someone can take pride in owning (versus an apartment building that people are willing only to rent), you can make a profit, even when using a contractor's work instead of your own sweat equity.

Many people, on the other hand, do the work themselves. You don't have to be a professional painter or carpenter to improve a property. When I was in graduate school, I discovered that the president of my university bought older buildings and spent the weekends scraping and painting them. He got the chance to get out of his normal academic setting and take his mind off his work while adding value to his properties. Depending on how handy you are, you may want to do the same thing.

Real estate flipping is all about finding property that's undervalued, and sometimes a property may simply be undervalued because it's shabby. If you can find a home that has been underappreciated over the years and just needs some basic updates, you can create a new and exciting property to flip.

Chapter 11

Keeping Tenants
During a Hold

The time may come when you decide to have a tenant live in a building that you're holding before you flip it. Although tenants can be a blessing and a curse, the income derived from them can be rather handy. It can cover or partially cover the expenses you'll incur while holding the property, such as repair, maintenance, improvements, taxes, insurance, and interest. Obviously, the more expenses your rents cover the better, and if you earn a profit during that time, that's better still. It's certainly possible that you'll get a free ride during this period, and you'll essentially get to use your tenants' money to build wealth. But how do you deal with tenants without creating a lot of hassle?

Working with tenants is a skill people flipping real estate should develop. You'll encounter some of the nicest people you'll ever meet, a lot of "average Joes," and some genuine scoundrels. You'll have to deal effectively with each type. How? That's what this chapter is all about.

What You Need to Know

When you are the owner of a residential property, you will have to become knowledgeable in such topics as . . .

- Monitoring cash flow
- Controlling expenses
- Filing tax returns
- Working with local, state, and federal governments
- Tenant's rights
- Disclosures
- Maintenance and repair (and how to find reliable contractors to provide them)
- Your legal responsibilities as a landlord
- Accounting

Most of all, as the owner of a residential property, you will encounter all sorts of personalities, and you will simply have to learn how to handle each of them.

Knowing Your Obligation to Existing Tenants

I have always said, doing business is easy; it's people who make things difficult! After you negotiate the best price for a piece of property and purchase it, you may think the tough part of flipping real estate is over. But if you decide to hold the property for any length of time, you may decide to have people pay for the building (and all or a good chunk of your expenses during the holding period) by renting it out.

If renters are living in your building when you buy it, you've been given a real estate blessing. After all, you can continue to rent the property without the hassle of finding renters. On the other hand, because these tenants come along with the property, you also don't get to screen people as you want to, and you may have tenants who don't pay or are difficult to deal with. After all, the former owner sold to you for a reason!

Chances are, the renters in your new building understand that the building has been sold. And, chances are, they have some anxiety about that. They had a deal with the previous owner—whether in the form of a written lease or a verbal agreement—and they want to make sure you honor those agreements. They don't want their rents to go up, and they want to make sure you will take care of their units.

If you do have tenants—whether or not they have leases—and if they are residential tenants (as opposed to commercial or business tenants), you may have to follow some pretty stringent laws, concerning such topics as . . .

- The type of notice that's required to enter apartments to show units
- Whether you can ask for security deposits
- Whether interest is to be paid on security deposits

Keep in mind that written leases always survive a closing, meaning that they transfer from owner to owner to protect the rights of the tenant. Commercial leases are a little different from residential ones in that, in addition to paying rent, tenants may also pay utilities, a portion of the real estate taxes for the property, and common area maintenance (CAM) expenses.

Whether you're flipping a property quickly or keeping it for long term, before you buy, take time to find out whether leases are in place and how those leases read. And before you make an offer, include in your contract a clause and provision that the sale is subject to the review and acceptance of all leases that are currently in place (and you may find a variety of pretty strange leases).

You also may encounter situations such as a tenant who claims he or she prepaid rent to the landlord at below market rent and shows you a receipt that you will then have to verify with the previous landlord. Be sure to obtain a certification of closing from the seller as to who the tenants are (if any), what rent was paid, the amount of the security deposits, and when those deposits were received (this is important if you're required to pay interest on security deposits).

It is critical to know what your liability is if you don't return security deposits on time. In Chicago, the Tenant's Rights Ordinance provides that security deposits and interest must be returned to a tenant within thirty days. There is no gray area in Chicago if you make a mistake on security deposit interest calculation or refund. If someone gives you a deposit—whether it's a key deposit, security deposit, pet deposit, or whatever—the deposit must be returned in a timely fashion with the appropriate interest calculated. If it isn't returned in thirty days, the penalty that will be brought upon the landlord or property owner will be a multiple of the security deposit. Make sure that you become familiar with the laws and regulations on this subject in your area.

Form a Maintenance Team

Even if you plan on flipping your new acquisition in a relatively short period of time, you'll still be responsible for the building (and the safety and comfort of your tenants). You can expect some repair problems or at least regular maintenance duties. The previous owner may have someone on staff or on call or even a company on contract to handle these necessary chores. Find out. Don't assume that repair and maintenance will automatically continue. You may have to build your own maintenance team. Evaluate what company or individual you can afford and make sure that you've got someone ready to answer the calls when they come in, because they most assuredly will come in. Please remember not to be "penny wise and pound foolish." Do not skimp or shirk your responsibility to maintain a sound and safe environment for your tenants. In addition to being the right and legal thing to do, it's far easier to fix a small leak than pay for flood damage (possibly including tenant lawsuits) from a leak that's been ignored.

Get ready for all kinds of calls. Many of them will be legitimate. Some will be belligerent. And more than a few will be unnecessary. Still, you will have to deal effectively with them all and do your best to maintain a healthy relationship with your paying tenants. Here's just one example of what you can expect.

Recently I inspected one of my properties only to find that a tenant who had complained of not having enough heat in her unit actually had her heat turned up to 90 degrees on a moderate winter day. Right away I realized that no matter how we cranked up the heat, this lady would never be warm enough. The way she talked we thought the boiler had gone out. It hadn't, but we checked and double-checked and still, it wasn't warm enough for her in her apartment. We eventually realized that there was just no way to satisfy this lady. Even wearing a sweater and wrapped in a thick blanket, she still had to have the heat up in the sweltering range. Over the years she lived in my building she was always the first to complain but we always responded and made any repairs necessary when we found a problem or potential problem. On the other hand, she paid her rent and in other ways was a good tenant, so we did our best to make her comfortable and to attend to her needs. It is important to recognize that satisfaction may be abstract to some tenants—you'll never please everyone all of the time.

Your Relationship with Your Tenants

As the owner of a property (or properties), it's important to make your presence and interest known to your tenants. Set up a schedule for visiting each of your properties, or if that's impossible, establish a routine for your property manager or maintenance person to do the same. Tenants feel better when they know that someone is taking care of things, even when things are going smoothly—and even more when they're not.

Being seen as involved is helpful, but it is also important for you as an owner to see what is going on for yourself. "Management by walking around" is a method of doing business that has proved to be successful in many businesses, and especially in real estate. As an owner, you will see things from a different perspective than anyone else. For example, some minor repairs that your maintenance person might be planning for next week could become an immediate priority if you know that a potential buyer for the property will be coming to view it tomorrow.

A good landlord is more likely to have good tenants. Here are a few simple ways to build strong relationships:

- Pay interest on your tenant's deposit (a requirement in some states).
- Provide a maintenance request form.
- Explain basic maintenance, and encourage tenants to solve minor problems themselves by providing the necessary equipment.
- Give your tenants a typewritten sheet with emergency phone numbers, your phone number, the number of your maintenance person, emergency evacuation routes, tips on equipment and appliances, and any other information your tenants will find valuable.

Getting New Tenants

If you find yourself unable to find tenants for a building you own (or don't have the time to do so), you may want to enlist a rental agent to find tenants for you. The need for rental agents varies, depending on market conditions. If you have an apartment that has remained vacant for some time, you will probably find it in your best interest to pay a commission to an agent, rather than lose months of rent checks. For a rental agent to earn that commission, he or she should provide excellent service, and not merely go through the motions. In most areas, rental commissions are set at half a month's or a month's rent.

Sometimes, in order to gain a commission more quickly, a rental agent will embellish the features of the apartment or leave out details. This may result in getting the prospective tenant to sign the lease, but in the long run it will probably result in an unhappy tenant. You should provide the agent with a detail sheet; that is, a sheet for those interested in renting the unit that accurately describes what is being leased. You should also supply the agent with the credit form and application that you want to use to verify the tenant history and credit history. Once the rental agent leaves, you have the sole responsibility for dealing with the statements that the agent made to the tenant on your behalf.

Screening a Prospective Tenant

However you find a tenant—on your own or through an agent—here is what you should check to be sure you have found someone satisfactory:

- *References.* Your prospect should provide satisfactory references from landlords for the past three years.
- *Income and employment.* The tenant's household monthly income should be three times (or more) the monthly rent. Please verify that the prospective tenant has a permanent source of income.
- *Evictions.* The prospective tenant should have a clean record.

- *Criminal record*. You'd be amazed at how many people managing rental properties ignore this key issue.
- *Identification*. Your prospect should produce a valid social security card and one other source of identification, such as a driver's license.
- *Collections*. The applicant's record should be free of collections for the past year.
- *Credit*. The only way to know if a potential tenant has a good record of paying his or her bills is to check the credit history.

Special Considerations

As the owner of a residential property over a period of time, you will have to consider a number of things you won't have to consider with properties that you immediately flip. The following sections will tell you about some of them.

Keeping it close

The forty-minute rule mentioned in Chapter 5 for scouting properties is especially important when owning residential properties. Problems grow at exponential rates with distance. Suppose a tenant calls with a complaint about not having any hot water. If you are a short drive away, it's no problem to invest a few minutes to light a pilot on a water heater. If, on the other hand, you or your maintenance person has to drive two hours there and back, you've wasted half a day of valuable time or more. The closer you are to your property, the better.

The risks of single-family homes

A single-family dwelling is probably the most affordable investment, as well as the most manageable property, especially if you have little experience in property management.

However, you should realize that single-family dwellings can be a bigger financial risk if the property becomes vacant. Instead of merely losing one part of the rent income, as in a multifamily building with one vacant apartment, you will be losing *all* of the income. And even without a tenant living there, you will still have to pay for the mortgage, the taxes, and the upkeep. So, before a tenant moves out suddenly, make sure you can carry your financial responsibilities for as long as it will take to get a new tenant moved in and paying rent.

Evicting Tenants—Only If You Have To!

Tenants may choose to hold their rent from you for a number of reasons:

- They believe the rent is too high and don't want to pay it.
- They believe you're not keeping up the unit very well and withhold the rent as a form of protest.
- They're moving soon and figure they'll just "use up" the security deposit as the final rent payment.
- They're trying to see how long they can get away with it.
- They just don't have the money to keep up with their monthly bills.

If you can address your tenants' concerns, you may be able to rectify the situation. But you may, in the end, have to forcibly evict one or more of your tenants. If you have never dealt with a forcible eviction, contact an attorney to find out what procedures you can follow (based on laws in your area) to evict a tenant quickly and easily.

The most important part of the process is giving notice. A "notice" is an official communication of a legal action or of someone's intent to take a legal action. For example, as a property owner, you may need to move a bad tenant from your building, and a legal notice of termination is required. The notice must be served on the tenant. It shouldn't be left in the door or handed to a friend, although in some states it is permitted to give notice to a family member or to another tenant residing in the space. The safest procedure is to deliver the notice to the tenant yourself. Make sure you know the law. If, by law, a witness is required, but you present the notice without one, legally you haven't given notice.

Chapter 12

Converting to Condos

One of the ways to flip a property is to buy a multi-unit apartment building or other good-size building (like a warehouse) with the intention of converting it to condominiums. You can also take existing rental property you own (an apartment building, house, or other building) and convert it to condos.

A condominium (or condo) is an apartment that's owned by the person living in it. All of the owners also jointly own common space, like parking lots, walkways, lawns, pools or ponds, and so on. Often, they pay dues or some other fee to an elected condominium board (or condominium association), which takes care of planting, mowing, maintaining, and snowplowing. Because many apartment buildings are in bad shape, you may be able to get an entire property pretty cheaply (say, $1 million, though that probably doesn't sound cheap!) and convert it to condominiums by making improvements for another million dollars or perhaps less (condominium buyers expect plush properties) and selling the units for a grand total of $2.5 million. Not a bad profit!

Conversion Requirements

Condominium conversion is no easy task. The owner faces strict rules, regulations, and legal requirements, which vary from community to community throughout the country. The process can be expensive and time consuming. On the other hand, condo ownership is highly desirable for individuals and families. It's a rapidly growing market and can be a highly profitable one for someone interested in flipping real estate. Condo conversion is at least something you'll want to examine in detail.

Three elements make up a condo: (1) the dwelling area, (2) shared ownership of common areas, and (3) easements that allow all owners to share access with each other's utility companies and vendors. In addition to owning their units, condo buyers have an undivided interest in all the common areas. For the property to be legally defined as a condominium the word "condominium" must appear in the name of the development or in the legal papers creating the project.

I've heard condos described as a "box of air" and that's a pretty accurate description. Look at a high rise unit. It's really nothing more than a series of boxes of air stacked side by side and on top of one another. Mom and Dad buy their box of air and then move in the furniture, little Freddy, Freda, and sometimes even Fido. Legal requirements vary, but generally will include at least the following:

- A condominium declaration or rules for living in the association.
- A condominium budget showing the amount of each owner's assessment or proportion of assessment. In a condominium dwelling each owner is responsible for his or her share of expenses for maintenance and repair of common areas and this is paid in the form of a financial assessment.

- A survey showing how the condominium is divided according to the condominium's legal declaration.
- An engineer's report showing that the property is in sound condition. Any defects the buyers should be aware of must be noted.
- A builder's warranty to the buyers for any work done to the unit. This is presented at the closing.

When buying a building to convert to condominiums it's essential that you give it "the once-over" to determine its physical condition. Unless you're an expert in electrical wiring, mechanics, plumbing, construction, and the other building trades, you're much better off paying for a real expert to handle this task or to accompany you on your tour. Here's a list of must-inspect areas:

- Walls
- Roof
- Ceilings
- Floors/flooring
- Siding
- Plumbing
- Electrical systems/wiring
- Air conditioning system
- Heating system
- Elevators
- Lobby conditions
- Windows
- Doors
- Subsoil conditions
- Flood danger
- Fire danger (near heavily forested area)
- Common areas
- Appliances
- Cosmetic appearances

Your property may have other elements, such as a swimming pool or an atrium. Be sure to check everything and verify its condition.

Financing a Conversion

It is extremely unlikely that any building you purchase to flip by converting to condominiums will be in perfect shape.

Even buildings in good or excellent shape are often in need of repair, and all buildings are in need of continuing maintenance. Expect some construction needs that will require construction financing.

Construction financing is an entirely different kind of financing than a conventional mortgage note or line of credit. When you get a mortgage for a home you get the money for that home. When you acquire construction financing the bank lends you the money for the property and for the construction costs required to bring it in line with your plans. These costs break down into two areas. *Hard costs* are the costs of your rehab of the property, how much it will cost to carry the project to completion. In other words, the "bricks and mortar." *Soft costs* cover such areas as your architect, designer, planner, rental furniture, setting up a model unit, advertising, and any number of expenses not directly related to building costs. The bank or lending institution will require a detailed budget which must include figures for the acquisition and all hard costs and soft costs.

People who are not in the real estate business look at a construction project, such as a conversion to condominium, and think the developer is writing a monthly check to the bank to cover all his or her expenses. If that were the case no one could afford any serious construction at all. There's a term you need to learn—*interest reserve*. It's a budgetary amount the bank adds to your debt with them every month. For example, if I were to buy a $1 million property with added hard costs of $500,000 and soft costs of $100,000, my total budget would be $1.6 million. At 5 percent, a loan of that size requires interest of $80,000 per year.

But am I using all of that $1.6 million at one time? The answer is no. I may need only $50,000 to get the rehab started. Later I will draw different amounts at different times. So, I'm not using all that money all the time. Naturally, I'll pay the full amount over time, but through interest reserve the bank doesn't demand that I send them a monthly check for the full amount of interest owed. The interest becomes part of the aggregate of what I owe.

Spiffing the Place Up

You also will have to deal with contractors and subcontractors to do the renovation work for you. Refer to the section in Chapter 4 on evaluating and choosing contractors for information on what to consider in assembling your team for a condo conversion project.

Whether you're converting a three-unit or twenty-unit building, the legal and practical requirements will probably be the same: reviewing contracts, making sure that the contractors fulfill their legal obligations to you, ensuring that work is completed on time, and attending to the qualities of the property that your buyers will require.

Understanding the Rights of Existing Tenants

Dealing with tenants in a condominium conversion is a sensitive issue. According to the ordinances of your city or county, you probably have to meet some legal requirements for giving adequate termination notice (that's another way of saying, "kicking them out") so that you can begin doing condominium conversion work. Again, depending on the laws in your area, you probably have to give your tenants the first right to buy the units in which they currently live or else extend their leases appropriately. Appendix E gives an example of the type of notice you will have to give to all tenants before engaging in a conversion to condominiums.

Be sure you understand the laws and obligations in your town so that you won't be caught in noncompliance and face heavy penalties. You can't claim that you just "didn't know" when you're standing before a judge after a tenant brings a case against you for violation of tenant ordinances.

Chapter 13

Selling Your Real Estate

O bviously, successful flipping requires successful selling. The process is pretty basic—simple really. That doesn't mean you can sail right through it without doing your homework, paying attention to detail, and keeping on your toes at all times. Selling is a strange and fascinating dance of allied and opposing forces. The buyer wants what the seller has, and the seller wants the buyer to have what he or she is selling. But, each also wants to get the best price possible, so there is inevitable conflict. Perhaps conflict is too strong a word, but realize that even though there will be a lot of "give" in the process, you will inevitably experience a good bit of "take." And that's okay. It's all part of the game.

As I said, the process is simple. There are four basic steps: (1) pricing your property right, (2) developing a marketing plan, (3) qualifying your buyer, and (4) closing the deal. That's all. Now let's see if I can make this simple process as easy for you as possible.

Step 1: Pricing Your Property

If someone offered you a $20 bill for $15, you'd take it, right? That's what real estate flipping is all about: buying real estate below value and selling it at or above the market value. This means that, before you buy, you need to have a good evaluation of the value of the property (see Chapter 7). What that also means is that you should have thoroughly priced your property—the price you're paying, the estimated expenses you may incur, and the potential market value (selling price)—the day you bought it. If you're paying $150,000 for a $200,000 property and you figured that your buying and selling expenses would run $20,000, you know you still stand to make $30,000.

How pricing works

On the game show called *The Price Is Right,* contestants try to win prizes by guessing the prices. The man or woman closest to the right figure wins. Pricing real estate is a somewhat similar game, although a very serious one with the prizes for either the buyer or seller running into tens or even hundreds of thousands of dollars. The seller has to guess the right price for the property and the guess had better be on target. Too low and you lose money. Too high and you'll lose your sale. The buyer has to guess the lowest price the seller will accept.

To take some of the guesswork out, you'll need to pretty well establish the probable sale price when you first look at the property. Sure, market forces, changes in the economy, changes in the community, and other factors may affect the eventual price, but you still have to make the best possible educated guess as to the potential market value of that land, building, or property before you make the purchase.

You don't want to overprice or underprice the property so that you put yourself in a deal that will only haunt you at the end. The more you flip properties the better you'll get at pricing. Your ability to make sure the price is right develops from your ongoing studies of the marketplace, from your research with other real estate professionals, and by developing your intuitive abilities. How are comparable buildings priced in the same area? What do your friends and associates in real estate and business think of the market trends? Where is the city moving? What does a professional assessment tell you? Is the area on the move, in decline, or bouncing back from a decline? Are stable families or businesses moving into the community or is it being taken over by gangs, crime, and people who have given up on life? Where are the prices in the area moving—up or down?

Rules of thumb for pricing

You'll find no absolutes for pricing. Every deal, even in the same municipality or neighborhood, is different. Still, there are rules of thumb that apply to every situation. First, you'll want to have two firm figures in mind: top dollar and bottom dollar. Top dollar is the amount of money you'd really like to make off the sale. It's not a pie-in-the-sky dream, but a realistic assessment. Bottom dollar is the lowest amount for which you will sell. If the buyer makes an offer below that point you'll walk away from the deal. For example, let's suppose you've purchased a small warehouse for $750,000. Your research and your intuition tell you that the best price you can hope for is $950,000. That's your top dollar. That same research and intuition plus your own financial and business needs tell you that you can sell and still make a decent profit at $855,500. That's your bottom dollar.

Second, understand that the range from top to bottom in most cases is about 10 percent. This rule of thumb may or may not apply in your situation. Local, regional, and national economies rise and fall, and pricing generally must accommodate those changes. In hot real estate markets where there is a lot of demand for property, you can often adopt a very firm pricing strategy and set your high and low price within a very small range, even less than 10 percent. I've seen some situations where the demand was so high that properties were selling way above what I considered market value. In depressed markets you'll probably have to create a more flexible strategy, perhaps more than 10 percent between your high and low price. The 10 percent rule is a sound place to begin; then look carefully at your market, honestly evaluate your position, and adjust accordingly.

When your estimates are wrong

If your price is right and you get it that's great, but sometimes we guess wrong. We buy real estate to flip that just can't be flipped. People always make mistakes—I have and so will you. It's human nature and you'll probably find yourself paying more for a property only to discover that your initial estimates and calculations were way off base. It happens. When it does, the best thing to do is get out of the deal as fast as you can and move on to bigger and better opportunities. And the best way to get out of a real estate transaction is to keep lowering the price until you find a buyer.

Step 2: Developing a Marketing Plan

Too many people just starting out in real estate are intimidated by the phrase "marketing plan." They have visions of leather-bound reams of paper full of charts, graphs, statistics, reports, and recommendations being handed out around polished wooden tables in fancy offices and boardrooms. It's not all that complicated, folks. You can find any number of good books on marketing written in plain English especially for small business people. They're in your library, in your favorite bookstore, and they can be ordered through the mail and online. I'll show you the basics and you can take it from there.

Forget your ideas about complicated reports and marketing jargon and just stick to answering a few simple questions:

1. *Exactly what is my offering?* Define your property in specific terms that explain its condition and use or potential uses.

2. *Who is my buyer?* What kind of people or organizations can afford to buy my property? What are their needs and how can my property meet those needs? Should I stress size, adaptability, historic value, location, or some other feature? All those features and more may be genuine features, but which ones will motivate my buyer?

3. *Where are those buyers located?* Is my market local, regional, national, or international? If local, is it in a specific geographic area? For example, are my potential buyers primarily located in big offices in the downtown businesses or are they smaller investors scattered all over town?

4. *What factors will motivate the buyer to buy?* Am I flipping to another flipper? If so, then my buyer must think that he got a great deal or that this specific property meets his need. Am I selling to someone wanting the property for long-term use? If so, then I should consider that their long-term plan will allow them to pay me a handsome profit.

5. *How can I let potential buyers know of my offering?* What do they read, listen to, and watch, and which of these influences will have the most impact on them? Does the medium I choose to reach them match those habits? For example, you wouldn't advertise the sale of a golf course in a local pennysaver newspaper, nor would you print up a $25,000 four-color brochure to sell a small tin building in a depressed neighborhood. Which is the best marketing vehicle: newspapers, magazines, direct mail, direct sales, some other traditional vehicle, or something off the wall?

6. *What is my marketing budget?* How much can I afford to invest in advertising, public relations, or knocking on doors before I start having a negative impact on my future profits?

7. *What is the most efficient, effective, and timely schedule for my marketing plan?* What type of purchaser is

best suited for this property? Where should I advertise to find this buyer? How should I write my ad to attract the right purchaser?

If you can answer those simple questions, you can develop and implement a successful marketing plan.

Here's one more word of advice on marketing your property. Don't get thrown by your lack of knowledge about advertising, media buying, graphic design, or public relations. You can get a lot of help from the sales representatives in all these media outlets; just be sure to establish a few guidelines up front with everyone you deal with. The way to handle these people is to describe your ideal buyer and get them to show you specifically how their vehicle reaches that market and at what cost. Be sure to get the full story up front, and get it from all appropriate sales representatives. Then make up your mind and make your move. Just remember that the sales rep from the *Wall Street Journal* will assure you his or her publication is the ideal vehicle. And the rep from *Forbes* will say the same thing, as will the reps from the direct mail marketing company, the PR firm, and the local newspaper.

Step 3: Qualifying Your Buyer

You will run into a lot of unqualified buyers and they can eat your lunch. An unqualified buyer will not come up with the necessary financing and will find some excuse for backing out at the last moment. You may not lose any capital, but dealing with unqualified buyers still costs you a lot in terms of your valuable marketing time, which could have been invested with better candidates. Plus, you could also lose on attorney or other fees, loan interest, and other expenses.

A qualified buyer is someone with a contract and a check. That's it. Period. No one, no company or organization, no group of investors is a qualified buyer until he, she, they, or it presents you with a contract and a check. Anyone else is just looking. Some may be just shopping around and others may be quite serious, but they're not qualified buyers.

Think of yourself when you purchased your building. The buyer for your property should have the same qualifications you brought with you. What did you have? You had a contract, which included the price, closing date, amount of earnest money, financing contingency, time for inspection, attorney's name, attorney review period, and any other terms and conditions you wanted to impose on the deal. You also arranged your financing in advance and therefore had a check. Your buyer should meet those same conditions.

Remember the sequence that buying a property takes:

1. Find a property you're interested in.
2. Make an appointment to see it.
3. Write a contract to make an offer.
4. Negotiate with the seller for a different price or terms (if the offer isn't accepted).
5. After the contract is accepted, have your Realtor or attorney review it.
6. Inspect the property.
7. Obtain or finalize financing.
8. Set a closing date.
9. Close and take possession.

There should be very little or no variance from this outline. Just as you were able to follow these steps, any qualified buyer should be able to do the same. If anything seems out of place, it probably is, and you probably don't have a qualified buyer.

What about the appearance, attitude, and general demeanor of potential buyers? Often you can make pretty sound judgments by such external matters. I know the seller of a small property who was approached by someone who clearly wasn't and would never be a qualified buyer. The man told the seller that he was divorced and currently living with a friend because he couldn't afford his own apartment. He was out of a job and had no prospects, but expected to get an interview in the immediate future. He had no savings, was driving a borrowed car, and wanted to know how little the seller would take for the property. Not all potential buyers are this open or obvious.

On the other hand, you really can't tell a book by its cover. I've encountered numerous millionaires and multi-millionaires who earned their fortunes from the ground up. Some began as roughnecks in the "oil patch." Others were ranchers who began as cowboys or ranch hands, or industrialists who began their careers on the shop floor. Many of these people still dressed as if they were blue-collar workers. Someone who has to spend part of the business day inspecting an oil well in the swamp or in a west Texas dust storm won't always be wearing a dress suit and highly polished shoes.

Ask the potential buyer if he or she has arranged financing. "This property is selling for $X. Have you qualified for that sum?" There's nothing wrong with asking that question. You're running a business. If the answer is yes, and it can be verified by the potential buyer's bank or other lending institution, you can proceed with some confidence. Don't completely blow off someone whose answer is no. He or she still might qualify and get the necessary financing. Just realize that at that moment you are not speaking with a qualified buyer.

Step 4: Closing the Deal

Here comes the fun part. Closing not only will provide you with the profit you have waited for, but you will experience both satisfaction when you see the process work and a let-down knowing that it's over. Remember, the closing is only as good as the check that the borrower brings to the table.

Finding loopholes in the buyer's contract

If it looks like a duck, quacks like duck, and swims like a duck—it's a duck. The same is true with a loophole. If it looks like a loophole, it's a loophole. If you see anything unconventional in a contract, chances are, your potential buyer is going to get out of the deal and get the earnest money back, while you're not going to be compensated for your time and expenses. You're not interested in people on a fishing expedition; you're there to sell real estate, so if you see or hear anything that's questionable, pass on this buyer and move on to someone else. Don't be tempted by a signed contract if, in the end, the deal will cost more than it's worth.

A contract contains several basic elements to evaluate:

- Names and addresses of the seller and buyer, and the address of the property
- A definition of the property with terminology specific to that property
- The price of the property
- Terms and conditions of the sale
- The amount of the down payment
- Mortgage and financing terms
- Date of possession
- Attorney approval clause
- Inspection period clause
- Closing date

There may be any number of additional clauses imposed by the buyer. These run the gamut from sensible to ridiculous. I once had a contract on a property contingent upon whether a piano would fit through one of the doors.

Loopholes are simply devices people use to get out of

a contract, and they can work for you or against you. Any contingency, any clause, or virtually any element of a contract can become a loophole. Some are exercised legitimately during the process and some are set in there as "land mines" to give the buyer or seller an edge or an easy way out. Be particularly sensitive of any clause that is subjective, and is something that is open to interpretation, because the interpretation may not be in your favor. The mortgage contingency can be a loophole, as can be the inspection contingency, the attorney approval contingency, due diligence, or any contingency at all. Often many loopholes are built into the same contract. Watch for any language that states the buyer must approve of something. If it's a subjective approval then it's probably a loophole.

Here's an example of the many things that might have to go right on the road to a signed contract. I have a meeting scheduled with a city alderman about a property I'm hoping to lease. It's a retail space in a retail section of town, but it's an ideal location and property for a community theater group's performance theater and rehearsal hall. This is a win/win situation for all concerned—if it ever comes together. The theater group won't lease from me until it acquires the appropriate building permits and licenses. Much of this is contingent upon the approval and cooperation of the alderman. Assuming the plan gets his approval, the group will then have to get an approval from the neighboring businesses. There is a long list of contingencies attached to this project. If for any reason the buyers decide to back out of the deal, any one of those contingencies could become a loophole. When dealing with contracts, remember the adage "it ain't over until it's over."

Then again, loopholes can be an *advantage* to the real estate flipper—as long as they're your idea. I use them all the time. If I see a property I want and I believe I can flip, but I want to tie it up until I can find a buyer, I'll put in my loopholes. Each contingency drags out the process, which in this case is in my favor. When I find my buyer and structure a contract, I take the opposite approach and avoid as many loopholes as possible.

Asking for earnest money

Many years ago, it was determined that something called "consideration" has to be involved in completing a real estate transaction: Something has to be given to you (the seller) in a material way that shows that the buyer is committed to proceeding with the sale and that you're serious about selling. Without consideration we'd have a whole lot more contracts falling through at the last minute. Earnest money makes the buyer aware of the seriousness of the contract, that he or she is making a commitment, and failure to follow through will be costly.

Now here's a simple translation: Consideration is money. Although I once heard a story in which someone tried to use golf balls as consideration, you are going to want money. A buyer must be able to provide you with cash to put in an escrow account that's held by a title company, your attorney, or by you to show in good faith that he or she wants to buy your property. This up-front deposit—usually given as a money order or certified check along with the contract—is called earnest money. It is money given to you "in earnest" upon the signing of a contract to close the deal, and is usually $1,000 to $2,500. Sometimes, an additional 5 to 10 percent of the purchase price is also requested after the contract has been reviewed by the attorney and is pending financing and closing. The acceptance of earnest money is a critical juncture for you: Accept it, and you indicate your intent to sell the property to that specific person. Reject it, and you're communicating that you won't be selling the property at that price to that person. I suggest an effective halfway alternative. Hold off on depositing the check until you are sure you are completely comfortable with the deal. If you change your mind or a better offer comes along, you aren't legally or morally out of line in giving back the earnest money. If you don't make the deposit you haven't officially accepted the money. If you're happy with the deal, then make the deposit right away and move on.

If a buyer wants you to accept a contract without earnest money, walk away. If he or she can't get enough cash for earnest money, this buyer will have trouble getting financing. And if a buyer doesn't put down earnest money and wants to walk away from the deal, the buyer loses nothing, while you lose time and money.

When a buyer who puts up earnest money backs out of a deal, that money is usually forfeited to the seller. The seller can put it in the bank, invest it, or spend it as he or she wants. Buyers who have backed out lose the money and can say nothing about it. Well, they can say something, but they can't do anything. My most recent observation of someone losing his earnest money involved the sale of an estate house. The buyer put up $2,500 earnest money and waived attorney approval, inspection contingency, and mortgage contingency. He took every step in proper order, but when he received his mortgage he didn't like some of the terms. At the last minute he wanted to reduce the price by $15,000 so his payments would be more in line with his expectations. Of course, he didn't have a valid argument for doing that, particularly as he had waived all of his contingencies. He didn't close and he lost the $2,500 to the seller.

Disclosures to the buyer

The best way to sell property is "as is." That way, once you get the money and the purchaser has inspected the property and taken possession, you will have no further responsibility. In most states you will be required to provide a disclosure form, which may deal with such matters as the physical condition of the property and environmental concerns. It's only fair to let the buyer know the property has a leaky roof or a basement that tends to flood, or if it is located over an abandoned nuclear waste dump. A buyer has a clear right to be informed of any substantial condition that could have a detrimental effect upon the property, and the seller has a legal obligation to disclose any such matters.

Never try to hide a problem. Besides being illegal and wrong, it will irreparably tarnish your professional reputation. It's far better to disclose any problems up front and show that they were repaired, and that the value of the property has therefore been enhanced.

Evaluating the offer

When that happy day comes and you are given an offer, look for the following in a written contract: a price plus the amount of earnest money to be deposited, a period of contingency for inspection and attorney review, and a closing date with the amount of additional earnest money to be deposited with you or an escrowee prior to closing. There really isn't much more to be considered unless special circumstances present themselves from your end, and you have already discussed these with your attorney in advance knowing how, what, and where your estate or business transactions have to be conducted.

Is the price within your top dollar/bottom dollar range? If you're just trying to get out of the deal, will the price at least allow you to break even? If you have to take a loss, is the loss acceptable considering your situation? Is the earnest money appropriate or is the buyer trying to get by with a small (and not very painful to lose) amount of money? Are the time frames for inspections and attorney review reasonable? Are they so long that they'll have a significant negative impact on your financial situation? Take a close look at all the contingencies. How many of them are legitimate and how many appear to be the loopholes mentioned earlier?

Selling property you don't yet own

Although some properties take years to flip, some take days—or even hours! On many occasions, I've looked for a buyer to flip to long before I've closed the deal on buying the property myself. But because you don't yet legally own the property, you have to be careful what sort of contract you sign.

Don't try to sell what you don't already own or have the capability to own. Keep in mind that even if you've signed a real estate contract to buy a piece of property, if you have yet to close, you don't own it. You own only the contract. If you advertise that real estate prior to closing and then sign a contract to sell to another party you could open yourself up to charges of fraud and misrepresentation. After all, you're offering for sale property that legally belongs to someone else. The way to protect yourself is to insert a clause in the sales contract that provides a legal loophole, an "out," should your contract to buy fall through. This is usually a simple phrase involving the words "contingent upon" followed by the conditions you need to protect your interests.

Perhaps you're thinking, "What can go wrong?" The closing date is set, you know that the seller's motivation is quite strong, the earnest money has been accepted, the title is clear, and the attorney approval and inspection approval have all been waived, so what could go wrong? For starters, the seller could die. That's right: If the seller dies before you close, the property sale may be tied up in probate or estate settling for years.

As a broker, I once had a listing for a bigwig attorney in Chicago. He accepted a contract from a buyer, a well-known Chicago politician. They got into an argument prior to closing and litigated an issue on the environmental representation that the buyer wanted but that the seller wasn't required to provide, according to the contract. In a nutshell, the buyer was going to flip the property and wanted more than the contract provided. He wanted to stall for time until his end buyer was in place, and he created a less-than-pleasant situation for the seller. Anyway, to make a long story short, they both died. That's right—both of them. The estates for both parties had to undo the contract obligations of the estates. Strange things can happen.

Some things you can't control, but you can control what you do and don't do. The bottom line in selling property you don't yet own is simple: Before you accept any offer to sell property that you are in the process of buying, (1) be sure you have a firm contract to buy that property and (2) be sure to write that "contingent upon . . ." loophole in your contract to sell.

Part Five

Expanding Your Flip

Part Five

Expanding Your Flipping Career

Chapter 14

Flipping Mortgage Paper

You don't have to acquire real estate to have real estate value. It's possible to buy and sell mortgages, and many smart investors earn a good living flipping paper instead of land, buildings, or houses.

How Mortgages Work

Barron's Real Estate Handbook (Barron's Educational Series, 2001) defines a mortgage as "a written instrument that creates a lien upon real estate as security for the payment of a specified debt." What does that mean? Well, a written instrument is simply a contract. I agree to do this for that. You agree to do that for this. Let's shake hands and sign on the dotted lines. A lien is a charge against a property making it a security for the payment of the mortgage. For example, let's say you hired me to repair your roof. I performed the work according to the contract, but you refuse to pay for the work. I could get a lien against your property for the amount of money owed me. And security is simply the property that is collateral for the debt.

How does all this come together? A mortgage is an

agreement that obligates the buyer to pay back any money he or she has borrowed to acquire property. When you close on a piece of property you sign a lot of papers. They all relate to the mortgage and are known as the mortgage papers. The forms may reach an inch thick and you may get writer's cramp before you finish signing your name on the last line of the last page, but they really all say one thing: If you don't pay the money you've promised to pay, the bank or lending institution will foreclose on your property. The lender has a legal right to take away your property if you renege on the deal and they'll have the full backing of the court and all its police power.

Buying and Selling Mortgages

This is where flipping paper comes in. As an investor you can just buy the note, sell it for a higher price, and let other people proceed with the foreclosure. One of the real benefits of this process is that you buy the paper at a discount and use the basic rule of profit: buy low, sell high.

Here's how it works. Let's suppose a bank lends a borrower $100,000 to buy a house. The deal goes through, people move in, time moves on, and after a few years the balance due on that $100,000 is now $98,000. For whatever reason, the borrower stops paying on the mortgage. Perhaps the borrower lost work, had extraordinary medical expenses, or lost all his or her funds at the casino. Maybe the borrower is just a deadbeat (and a lot of deadbeats have a lot of money). You'll hear all kinds of reasons and rationalizations if you enter this area of real estate.

After repeated calls and letters the bankers realize that they're not going to get their money from the borrower. They also realize that foreclosing on a piece of property is a time-consuming and costly business. The job can also be emotionally challenging. Imagine foreclosing on someone who's lost a job or has a medical problem and can no longer pay the bills. Different institutions have different reasons at different times to sell the paper. It's in their best interest to sell the mortgage to a third party, get their money out of the deal, and move on. To attract buyers, the bank offers a discount. This discount is the highest figure the lending institution can negotiate and the lowest amount the third party is willing to pay for the paper.

The third party can then sell and flip the note for a quick profit or carry the judgment through foreclosure and become a property owner. Either way he or she makes money on the deal. For example, if you acquire the $100,000 note for a discounted fee of $80,000, that's like buying a dollar for eighty cents. And in buying paper you're buying a lot of dollars. The key is to make sure you can take financial advantage of the discount. Your $20,000 profit could easily be eaten up by legal fees and other obligations, such as the borrower declaring bankruptcy. Make sure you are certain of all costs or probable costs before you begin.

The Legal Process of Foreclosure

To get the process rolling, you first need to find a lender that wants to avoid going through the lengthy and time-consuming process of foreclosing on a piece of property. If the bank or other company has already received a judgment of foreclosure (meaning that, legally, the foreclosure can take place), you're way ahead.

That piece of legal paper is a decree from a court that one person owes a debt to another, stating the amount of indebtedness. For example, if one of your tenants fails to pay the rent due, as the landlord you could appeal to the court for a judgment against that tenant. You, as the person to whom the money is owed, would be the judgment creditor, and you receive the judgment. The tenant, the individual against whom the judgment has been made, would be the judgment debtor. A judgment lien is a claim by one person against the property of another resulting from a judgment. For example, suppose you put in a new parking lot for one of your apartment buildings. It makes the tenants happy, improves the view, and enhances your property's value. Then, for whatever reason, you refuse to pay the contractor. The contractor can go to court, establish the validity of the debt owed, and put a lien against your real estate.

If the lender has not obtained a judgment before you buy the mortgage, understand that before you or anyone else can proceed with the foreclosure, you must go before a judge. As with all legal proceedings, getting a judgment is a crapshoot. There are too many factors involved to guess the outcome in advance. That is why it is always best to have the judgment of foreclosure in hand before you buy the mortgage, or to sell the mortgage before one becomes necessary.

Chapter 15

Flipping Commercial Properties

You may choose to focus on residential properties (houses, townhouses, condos, and so on) and make a great profit flipping real estate. But if you want to expand your horizons, consider also looking at industrial buildings, inner-city business buildings, shopping centers, and so on. These properties, known as commercial properties, offer additional flipping opportunities for you.

Defining "Commercial" Versus "Residential"

Single-family dwellings, condominiums, co-ops, and town homes fall into the category of residential properties, because people live in them. Commercial properties, on the other hand, are buildings used for purposes other than dwelling—in other words, people don't usually live in commercial properties. Some examples include shopping centers, office buildings, golf courses, funeral homes, automotive repair garages, industrial buildings, and manufacturing plants. You do find some gray areas, however. Apartment buildings with two or more units are dwellings for someone, but if you own one of these properties as an investment, it's considered a commercial property for you.

Commercial uses of properties are defined by your city, township, or county, according to zoning ordinances. For example, a specific part of town could be zoned strictly for residential purposes, where people can build homes or other residential dwellings, but not commercial properties, such as a manufacturing plant. Other areas may be for commercial use, and you can't build a residential property there. Commercial uses may also be split into subcategories, such as industrial or light industrial. You can find out how a building is zoned from the Realtor representing the property or from city, township, or county officials.

Naturally, as an area grows and changes, its zoning ordinances change to accommodate the way the area is evolving. A downtown residential area can at some time become a commercial district, as people move to the suburbs. On the other hand, commercial zones could be converted to residential use as people move back to the city. One hundred years ago, a lot of manufacturing facilities were located in the heart of the city. With little or no room to expand horizontally, the industries were housed in tall buildings built in the "loft" style of architecture, meaning several floors. Huge freight elevators carried people, equipment, raw materials, and products from one floor to the next. The years following World War II brought a major flow of people from the city to the suburbs, and business people realized two key factors: The workforce was moving away, and businesses could be made more efficient if more business was conducted on a single floor. So, these downtown businesses followed the crowd and left the downtown, too. Naturally, this exodus left a lot of empty buildings, many of them in prime locations.

A lot of smart investors realized that these abandoned or underused buildings could be converted to places where people could live and work, as long as the buildings could be zoned as residential. This was positive in many aspects:

- The city got viable properties and, therefore, more tax revenues.
- People who like the buzz of the city could find quality housing near employment, cultural, and recreational activities.

These properties were, and frequently still are, very good opportunities for flipping. Just keep in mind that if you're looking at unused commercial buildings as potential residential properties, check out the zoning ordinances before placing an offer. Regardless of how prime a location may be or how much residential space is needed, if the zoning isn't there, you won't be able to sell your property as residential. You don't want to buy a building only to find that you can't resell it for residential use.

If a building you're interested in doesn't have the zoning you want, check with the city, township, or county to see whether you can get the area rezoned. Depending upon where you live, this process can be incredibly easy or an ordeal that you'd be better off passing up. The bottom line? Check around. Know what you're about to get into before you make a commitment.

Finding Commercial Flipping Opportunities

Finding commercial flipping opportunities is a bit more of a challenge than finding residential opportunities. That's simply because there are more people (and, thus, residential properties) than businesses (commercial properties). Homes, townhouses, and condominiums are more common than loft-style commercial buildings, plants, and other commercial properties. That doesn't mean opportunities aren't available. They are, and some of them are golden.

The way to find them is the same way you conduct other business: You network. Ask around. Talk to your friends, neighbors, attorney, accountant, and anyone you know in real estate. Take particular interest in any business that's downsizing and looking to make some money by selling off some of its unneeded real estate. Businesses also merge, move, or make other changes that leave them with unused property. Sometimes those businesses are more concerned with getting fast cash than getting top dollar, and you can find terrific flipping opportunities.

Opportunities in distressed properties

You can also find great opportunities in real estate businesses that have been mismanaged. Such businesses may own properties that have become distressed real estate. Don't let that term throw you. Distressed property doesn't automatically mean there's anything wrong with the real estate. More often than not, the problems were created by poor management—such as an ineffective property manager, property that costs more than the rent can sustain, or tenants not paying their rent—and not the real estate itself. (Naturally, you should thoroughly investigate any property you're considering buying to make sure it doesn't have any inherent problems.) The poor management of these properties translates directly into high vacancy rates and loss of equity.

If the rents can't be collected or if there just aren't any renters, the owner may be looking to bail out of his or her financial dilemma. I look for good properties under bad management because I know my own capabilities for managing real estate investments. If I can find a sound property with unsound management, I can usually buy it and turn it into a going concern or a quick profit.

Where's the next good neighborhood?

Real estate investors are always looking for more property and more profit. Some owners continue to buy real estate and add to their portfolio knowing that they'll make money on a cash flow basis or on the appreciation of the property over time. Commercial flipping opportunities often present themselves in the category I call the next best neighborhood. Neighborhoods rise and fall and rise again, and smart investors are always asking themselves where the next hot spot will be.

That hot spot is always moving around. Think about how the communities around you have changed during the past half century. Fifty years ago, people flocked to the city for a chance at finding a better opportunity than what they found in rural living. Yet not too long ago, many families abandoned traditional city life and fled to the suburbs. There were many reasons: good jobs, failing intercity government and support structures, or a desire for a less cluttered and slower-paced life. In recent years, however, a reversal of that pattern has emerged, as more and more people realize the benefits and charms of living in the city.

Think about all those changes. Think, too, about how many times you've heard, "Well, we never thought this neighborhood would come back, but it sure did." Many of our parents and grandparents fled living in the city, thinking it was the worst place possible to raise a family. In some cases, they were right. But many of those places today have gentrified and are active, thriving, and healthy communities. All this change means there is great opportunity for flipping, provided you put yourself in the right place at the right time.

There's no specific roadmap. To a considerable degree, flipping depends upon the use of your intuitive abilities and your willingness to listen, learn, and apply what you learn. Use those abilities to help you find the next good neighborhood.

Finding Diamonds in the Rough

Rogers Park is a lovely neighborhood, a lakefront area within the city of Chicago. It is bordered on the north by the city of Evanston, home to Northwestern University. The area was built in the early 1900s and is full of large apartment buildings located very near one another. The neighborhood probably has the largest concentration of multiunit apartment buildings in the city. At one time, it was a very nice neighborhood populated by families who maintained their properties, respected their neighbors, and took pride in the community.

Things began to change in the 1960s, as these families moved to the suburbs of Skokie, Morton Grove, Highland Park, Northbrook, and Buffalo Grove. As they moved out, others moved in, and most of these folks were lower-income families. Often, the new tenants had trouble paying their rents. Many real estate owners left the area for greener pastures. Other problems arrived. Houses of worship closed. Retail sales suffered. Shopping centers in the suburbs attracted many other businesses out of the neighborhood or forced them to close. The area went into a serious decline. Rogers Park became a haven for drug dealers and other criminals, and this had a negative impact on everyone in the community. Despite its great location and many attractions, this wasn't a place you'd want to bring your family.

As a young Realtor out to make his mark in the world, I started to buy and sell properties in Rogers Park. This was at the height of the abandonment phase in the area's history. Many of the properties were boarded up or were partially boarded up. Units were selling between $5,000 and $10,000 each. (At that time, investors were paying those amounts, figuring they could then sell the properties for $20,000.) That was considered top dollar for buildings in that area, because the area could be flat-out dangerous to be in or around.

Things change. Today, apartment buildings in Rogers Park sell for $100,000 per unit. Neighborhoods like Rogers Park are the new frontier of real estate. It's bouncing back and becoming an area with town homes and condos. Investors started buying buildings, getting low-income financing, and fixing up their properties. They knew that people would be attracted to such a great location. Although I wish I had invested much earlier, a year ago I bought a nice commercial mixed-use property and I'm happy with the income it produces.

The same type of recovery came to another Chicago neighborhood called the South Loop. Its story illustrates many of the things you could face as someone flipping real estate, in particular the importance of getting into a market at just the right time. In 1983, Chicago got some great news: It had the possibility of becoming the site of the World's Fair. That's really big business, and a lot of people would have benefited from the influx of capital. Harold Washington was the new mayor, but unfortunately for Mr. Washington and a lot of Chicagoans, a majority of the city council opposed everything he wanted to accomplish. If the mayor was for it, the council was against it. The stalemate developed into something the media called the "Council Wars."

Meanwhile, investors who anticipated the World's Fair were buying vacant land and empty buildings in the area where the event was to take place. The area was no longer servicing Chicago's business community, because many of the businesses that had been there had relocated to the more profitable suburbs. So, some of this property could be purchased for as little as fifty cents or a dollar a square foot. Investors bought a lot of that property. Prices increased. People were making a lot of money—until the "Council Wars" stopped the World's Fair. The people owning property in the area discovered they'd paid a lot of money for virtually useless land.

Eventually, however, developers realized that this area just outside Chicago's loop was a great location for residential development. Then came a frenzy of buying and selling commercial and industrial properties and loft buildings.

Today, Chicago's South Loop is a popular and thriving community. Its buildings have won design awards throughout the world.

My point is that there are many places like Rogers Park and the South Loop. People turn up their noses at them, but these people are turning down a good deal. There are a lot of places that people, some of them wise investors, want to avoid like the plague. However, only a few fortunate and farseeing people can recognize the diamond in the rough.

Financing for Commercial Real Estate

Commercial real estate has different financing requirements than does residential real estate. First, it often requires a 20 to 30 percent down payment, which may be more than residential properties require. In other ways, however, financing commercial properties is easier than financing residential ones. For example, if the property is to be used to produce income, the lender looks at how much the income of the property can help pay for the mortgage. The lender also examines vacancy rates and looks at what sort of income the property will generate if it isn't leased at 100 percent capacity. The lender wants to make sure you can carry the mortgage, utilities, insurance, taxes, fees, and other costs, too.

If you're serious about flipping real estate, you need to get serious about your banking and lending (see Chapter 4). Chances are, you'll need a stronger and more sophisticated lending relationship than if you were purchasing a residential property. This is because, with commercial property, you're acquiring larger and more expensive properties, which means you need a large line of credit or more equity to buy commercial property in a timely and seamless way.

Even if you're not planning on making a commercial purchase in the near or relatively near future, if you think you want to flip commercial properties, immediately start forging strong banking relationships (that's right—with more than one bank, just to keep your options open!). Often the banker with whom you have a strong, long-term relationship can pull a few strings you couldn't pull on your own to help the process along. When you know how much financing will be at your disposal, you can start looking at potential commercial properties.

Make sure your mortgage does not have a prepayment penalty (also called a yield maintenance penalty). What these penalties do is charge you the full amount of interest on the loan, even if you pay the loan off early. When flipping property, you want to make sure you can pay the debt off early (if, for example, you can flip the property) and not pay a steep penalty.

When you flip the property to someone else, make sure your buyer can also obtain a loan to purchase commercial real estate. Verify that your buyer really does have the full down payment and will be in a position to close the deal in a timely fashion.

Commercial Property and the Marketplace

If you're planning on purchasing and flipping commercial properties, you have to know what you're getting into; that is, you have to know and understand the marketplace. Start immediately. Get advice from your attorney, accountant, and real estate professionals, and also do your own serious research. And don't forget your research is an ongoing process. Markets change and you'll have to keep up with the changes, so don't assume that after you've researched an area, your work is done. Keep up with the buying, selling, and value of real estate in the area(s) you've targeted.

Like most people, you're probably relatively familiar with the ins and outs of residential property. You've probably bought—and maybe sold—at least one residential property. You may not, however, have ever even looked at a piece of commercial real estate! But even with limited experience, you can learn to identify potentially good deals.

To limit your chances of making a mistake, be sure to include a due diligence clause in your contract. This clause allows you a stated period of time in which to inspect the property before you fully commit to the agreement. This gives you time to make sure the property is sound and that you have a reasonable chance of flipping it in a reasonable period of time for a decent profit. The clause may read something like this: "The seller will allow the buyer sixty days in which to complete due diligence inspection of the real estate to include all aspects of the property." It may continue with: "If the buyer so desires to extend the due diligence an additional sixty days the buyer will notify the seller in writing or by facsimile no later than the fifty-fifth day of the first due diligence period." This is just an example. You'll have to adapt your clause to your specific needs. However you word it, be sure the due diligence clause allows you time to conduct your research and property inspection while tying up the property so that another buyer doesn't take it. If everything checks out to your satisfaction, you can then complete the arrangements and close the deal. Even with the best-appearing opportunity, you never really know how long it will take to flip the property or how much profit you'll actually make. A due diligence clause will give you the time you need to make a sound financial decision.

Chapter 16

Understanding the Tax Implications

Taxes on real estate come in a number of forms, from property taxes to taxes on the income you earn from flipping properties. This chapter addresses primarily the taxes you pay when you profit from the sale of real estate, and also gives you tips and techniques for avoiding paying on income from the sale by quickly buying another property.

Paying Your Property Taxes

Every municipality (the government unit for the area in which you live) requires property owners to pay a tax for the privilege of owning real estate. Every year, the property you own is assessed a fee, and that fee is used to help pay for schools, sewer systems, parks and recreation, and other infrastructure. You have a legal obligation to pay the city, county, or state your fair share of taxes during the time you own those properties.

Property taxes (also called real estate taxes) are fairly easy to understand for most people getting involved in real estate. A bill arrives every year (sometimes semiannually, dividing the tax bill into two portions). It shows the value of your property based on its current assessed value as well as the amount you owe. This is money that comes directly out of your pocket. Whether or not you think it fair, you still have to make the payments. If you refuse or fall behind in your payments, the taxing body can put a lien on your property. In some cases, it has the right to take your property from you.

The focus of this chapter is not on property taxes, because they are usually straightforward and inescapable. Instead, the remainder of this chapter focuses on the taxes you pay when you sell and profit from real estate.

The Two Levels of Taxation on Your Real Estate Profits

The more successful you are in flipping real estate the more taxes you will pay. It's the law of the jungle, and there's no escaping it. It is essential that you fully understand the tax implications of buying and selling real estate so that . . .

- You pay the minimum amount of taxes.
- You don't get into trouble with the IRS or any other taxing body.

Real estate is taxed at two levels: capital gains and ordinary income.

Ordinary income tax

Ordinary income tax is applicable to real estate flippers who purchase property for the express purpose of resale at a profit (which, of course, you want to do!). In this way, you're no different from a car dealer, grocer, or retail store: You buy and sell inventory. It's just that your inventory is in land, buildings, and properties. Generally, when you buy and sell properties, your profits are taxed at the ordinary income rate, which, depending on the tax laws in effect at any particular time, can be quite high—even over 40 percent, particularly if you have to pay state or local income taxes along with federal taxes.

During the time between the purchase and the sale of your property, if you collect rent from tenants, the rent is also considered ordinary income. Naturally, you'll be investing in your property to make necessary repairs, conduct maintenance, and to perhaps spruce it up for a faster sale during the same time. Those outlays of cash are considered as expenses and are not taxable (they can be deducted from income to reduce taxable income). Find out more in the "Income and Losses During the Hold" section later in this chapter.

Capital gains

Capital gains is just a fancy way of referring to the profit you earn on the sale of property. While ordinary income is income derived from the *operation* of real estate, capital gains is the profit derived from the *sale* of real estate. For example, suppose you purchase a building for investment and pay $25,000. Later, you sell that building for $30,000. The $5,000 profit can be reported on your income tax as a capital gain. (Of course, you could lose money on the deal, which would be reported as a capital loss.) According to the IRS tax code, you have to own your property for, generally, at least six months to a year (check with your accountant or tax attorney) to take advantage of capital gains. The beauty of capital gains is that the rate can be much lower than the tax rate for ordinary income—perhaps even 20 percent or less, depending on the current tax laws.

You can also avoid paying capital gains altogether by purchasing a property of greater value as soon as you sell your existing property. Here's how it works:

1. You purchase your property for resale.
2. You find a buyer, make the sale, and pay off all

your costs, debts, fees, and expenses.

3. Instead of taking your profits from the sale you place them in the care of a third party, usually a local lending institution or title company.

4. The third party holds your funds in escrow while you hit the streets to find another property to buy.

5. You purchase the new property.

6. You avoid paying capital gains taxes on the first piece of property.

I expand on this tool later in this chapter in the "Understanding the 1031 Exchange" section.

Income and Losses During the Hold

If you buy a property and rent it, the tenant provides you with income during the period you're holding that property. Income is good, of course—it provides funds for maintaining, repairing, and making your property more attractive, as well as paying any mortgage on it. Getting income for those expenses is much better than digging into your own pocket! It certainly makes the entire process of flipping easier and more manageable. The downside of rental income, though, is that it's taxed at the ordinary income rate. That rate is usually twice the rate of capital gains and there's no way to convert income of this nature into capital gains.

However, you may be able to offset some ordinary income taxes or even have a capital loss because of the expenses incurred in maintaining your property. For example, if you receive $5,000 income from the property, but your expenses on that property amount to $6,000, you have incurred a $1,000 loss for the year. This loss can be applied in a limited way to your ordinary income. It can be applied 100 percent to the capital gain you'll receive when you sell your property. When you do the calculations, the loss from ordinary income from your property is offset by the gain you made from the sale.

Work closely with an accountant who understands rental income. He or she will know how to calculate income from rents and can help you understand how the income from your tenants will affect your overall income during the time period you are holding your building.

If you are new to real estate, get to know the National Association of Realtors (NAR). You can find it easily on the Internet through its Web site at *www.realtor.com*. The organization does a lot of good for the real estate industry, Realtors, and the people who benefit from Realtor services. The NAR was instrumental in passing a law in the late 1990s that allowed real estate professionals to use losses experienced in real estate ventures to offset their income dollar for dollar. A real estate professional is defined as someone who spends more than 50 percent of his or her time actively selling real estate, managing real estate, or in any real estate activity. This is a significant benefit compared to the status of other professionals who own real estate as part of an investment portfolio or who receive income from real estate, but who are not considered real estate professionals. Let me explain.

Prior to 1986, people investing in real estate could use the losses on their real estate activities to offset their overall income. That's a terrific tax advantage. For example, let's say you earned $300,000 and invested as a limited partner in real estate as a 10 percent owner of a large office building. If the property incurred a loss due to depreciation—and not a loss based on the property expenses costing more to operate the property than the income received—then you will have an accounting loss at the end of the year. Remember, depreciation is something that the government throws into an equation to compensate for the normal wear and tear that property experiences over time. That loss due to depreciation is a loss any investor could use to offset ordinary income.

President Reagan initiated a number of tax reforms during the early 1980s to stimulate the economy. One of them was called the "accelerated depreciation method" which allowed investors to depreciate a property with a high front-end load or accelerated basis during the early years of ownership. Depreciation didn't have to be spread equally over the lifetime of the investment. That was a pretty good deal and a lot of people jumped at the opportunity.

Things change. Many of the reforms worked and the economy started rolling again. In 1986, that which the government gaveth, the government tooketh away. The accelerated depreciation method and the use of losses against ordinary income were eliminated or phased out over a period of five years. The reason was simple. The federal government wanted more money. The financial advantages provided to investors were taken away so the government wouldn't lose the possible tax revenue.

Those were very shortsighted moves. The government didn't realize or didn't want to realize the catastrophic events that would follow with the elimination of such powerful financial tools. What followed was like a row of dominos falling. Investors had for years been borrowing money from banks, savings and loans, and insurance companies. Much of that investment capital had been put into real estate. Financial institutions operate on lending money and then getting it paid back with interest, but the changes in the tax rules and regulations threw a monkey wrench into the works.

Since the borrowers could no longer use losses to offset income, their financial situation deteriorated. Many of them were unable to pay back their loans. Many of these loans fell into the category of no-recourse loans. When the banks couldn't get their loans paid back, the money basically disappeared. The investors didn't have it. The banks didn't have it. Many of the nation's financial institutions didn't have the financial reserves to weather the storm. The federal government had to establish the Resolution Trust

Corporation that operated from 1989 to 1994. The RTC was given the responsibility of disposing of banks, their assets, and even their furniture, equipment, and artwork. The idea was to get money back into circulation to replace the deposit amounts that were federally insured. The changes in the once-favorable tax code had created a financial disaster of enormous proportions.

However, thanks to the National Association of Realtors and its political action committee, full-time real estate professionals can once again use their losses and depreciation to offset their ordinary income. I use that advantage, and so can you. Realize that depreciation can no longer be accelerated and must be spread throughout the life of the property. This figure will vary depending upon whether it's residential property at 27½ years or commercial property at 39 years. These changes in favor of the industry are a reason you may want to consider leaving your day job for a career in real estate. The IRS has two categories of depreciation for real estate: one for residences and apartments—27½ years—and one for commercial property—39 years.

You should also know that the losses you will experience by being a real estate professional will not exclusively apply to ordinary income. They apply to capital gains, as well. When you do your taxes at the end of the year, the depreciation is subtracted out of the equation to account for the repairs that the owner would spend to maintain the property. Currently, you're allowed $3,000 per year in losses. Yet, if you lose $36,000 in one year, you can spread that loss over twelve years of income at $3,000 of loss per year.

Full-Time Professionals and Business Deductions

If your primary business, as defined by the Internal Revenue Service, is real estate, then you can deduct real estate losses from your personal income. This benefit is one result of the Revenue Reconciliation Act of 1993, which covers rental real estate activities (RREAs). If you qualify, your RREAs are not subject to limitation under the passive loss rules of the IRS. Passive loss is the loss that the entire equation of property ownership provides, the rent-expenses-depreciation costs, when the owner *does not* actively operate the property as his source of primary income or primary profession. But you do have to meet certain criteria. Your real estate business can't be a sideline or part-time affair, and the law requires that you be materially involved in real estate.

If you are working full-time in real estate, and not just doing the occasional flipping deal, your real estate commissions, wages, interest, and dividends are subject to income taxation. On the plus side, full-time real estate professionals can deduct their real estate losses at the end of the year. In other words, if the accounting from your property shows a loss due to expenses added to depreciation, you can deduct that paper loss from your professional income. Real estate is the only profession that allows that deduction to pass through.

Of course, you must always be aware that tax laws are changing all the time. Always consult your accountant before filing to make sure you're up to date on the latest changes.

Understanding the 1031 Exchange

Owning real estate affords you certain privileges depending on how long you hold your real estate. According to the IRS 1031 Rule, no gain or loss is recognized at all if property held for productive use or for investment is exchanged for property of a like kind that's either for productive use in trade or business or for investment. Like-kind property means property of the same nature or character, not necessarily the same grade or quality.

What does all this mean for real estate flipping? Here's an example: Suppose you purchase a property for $200,000 and hold that property for a period of from six months to a year. (Because of the fuzziness of some IRS guidelines, consult with your accountant as to how this period should be defined for your situation.) Now, suppose you sell that property and earn a $50,000 profit and you know that you intend to continue investing in real estate. You have two options: You could take that profit, put it in the bank, and pay your capital gains taxes; or, you could put IRS Rule 1031 to work for you.

Instead of placing that $50,000 into your bank, you put it into an exchange bank, a third party that will hold the funds in escrow. Exchange banks are easy to find—many local banks and title companies act as exchange banks. (Just be sure that this third party is legitimate and not your spouse or cousin!) After doing this, you have six months to buy another property. During the first forty-five days of that six months, you must designate up to three properties that you intend to invest in or buy. The government allows you this time because you may not have a specific property or properties in mind at the moment of the sale of the original property. Therefore, you get some time to look around.

A month and a half may sound like a lot of time, especially in a hot market, but the adage "time flies" was never truer than in real estate. Consider that the closing period for flipping real estate is usually forty-five to sixty days after the property is under contract. I strongly advise that the moment you know you're going to sell your property, you get out there and start looking for others.

After forty-five days, you can begin negotiating on which property you want to purchase, purchasing it within six months. Provided you close within six months of the original date you sold your original property, you can reinvest your $50,000 held in escrow into another property and not pay taxes on that capital gain until that next piece of property is sold. If you hold the next piece of property for a period of between six months to a year or longer, when you sell that property you can buy something else.

Here are the basic rules of the 1031 Exchange:

- Designate your new properties within the first forty-five days.
- Close within 180 days (six months).
- Always buy a property for a higher price than the property you sold.

Taking advantage of the 1031 Exchange is a very sound way to build up your real estate empire. Here's a personal example. I bought a ten-unit apartment building in the 1990s for $420,000, with the idea of using it to generate income. The venture turned into a wonderful opportunity for flipping instead: After holding this property for a couple of years, I realized that it had appreciated in value far more than I was earning as income, so I sold it for $895,000. Although I had invested in maintenance, repair, and improvements I still had about $400,000 left over, and it would have been taxed as income.

Instead, I used that $400,000 to purchase, within the six months allowed under the 1031 Exchange, three properties with combined values exceeding $2.5 million. Three years later, one of those three properties sold. That sale generated enough profit to buy three more properties, again, within the six-month period allowed under 1031. I resold two of those properties within six months and now own two much larger properties—all this starting with my original purchase of that ten-apartment building. The value of that first $420,000 acquisition now exceeds $10 million.

That's how real estate flipping can work. I'm not a genius. If I can do it, so can you. And you can do it virtually anywhere in the country. The opportunities for real estate flipping are enormous and everywhere, but you can't win if you don't play. I have been able to build a sizeable estate in less than a decade. It generates wonderful income and has appreciated in value year after year. This may sound like a pitch from one of those late-night infomercials, but it's true. And it can be true for you, also.

Glossary

AAA tenants: The most creditworthy tenants as determined by a national credit rating service.

abandonment: The release of a claim or a right in a piece of property with the intention of terminating ownership and without giving it to anyone else.

abatement: A reduction in amount.

abnormal sale: A sale that is not typical within the context of the market; this can occur because of undue pressure on either the buyer or the seller or for some other reason. A foreclosure could be pending, a move out of state could be pending, or perhaps the property owner just cannot afford to keep the property.

absentee ownership: The owner of property does not physically reside on the property.

absorption rate: The percent of total real estate space of a particular type that can be sold or leased in a local market.

abstract of title: A history of the ownership of a parcel of land that lists transfer of title, rights, and liabilities.

accelerated depreciation: A method of depreciation for income tax purposes that increases the write-off at a rate higher than occurs under straight-line depreciation.

acceleration clause: A statement that says, upon default all of the principal installments come due immediately.

access: The right to enter and leave property.

accessibility: The ease with which one can enter and leave a property.

accrue: To accumulate.

accrued depreciation: Any diminishment of utility or value from the cost of an improvement on property.

acquisition: The process by which property ownership is achieved.

acquisition cost: The total cost of purchasing an asset, including closing costs and other transaction expenses added to the selling price.

acre: A measure of land equal to 43,560 square feet.

actual authority: A power that a principal has expressly conferred upon an agent or any power that is incidental or necessary to carry out the express power.

actual eviction: The violation of any material breach of covenants by the landlord or any other act that wrongfully deprives the tenant of the possession of the premises.

adjusted cost basis: The value of property for accounting purposes, equal to the original costs plus costs of any improvements less depreciation.

adjustments: In the market data approach to value, these are the additions and subtractions that are made to account for differences between market-comparable properties and the subject properties being appraised.

ad valorem: A prefix meaning "based on value"; most local governments levy an ad valorem tax on property.

advance: A fee paid before any services are rendered; in construction financing, the advance provides the builder with working capital.

adverse possession: A method of acquiring original title to property by open, notorious, and hostile possession for a statutory period of time; also referred to as *prescription.*

affidavit of title: A sworn statement by the seller that no defects other than those stated in a contract or deed exist in the title being conveyed.

after-tax cash flow: Cash received plus tax savings or minus tax liability of a project.

agency: A relationship in which one party (the principal) authorizes another party (the agent) to act as the principal's representative in dealing with third parties.

agent: One who acts for and in place of a principal for the purpose of affecting the principal's legal relations with third persons.

agreement: An expression of mutual assent by two or more parties.

agreement of sale: A contract between a purchaser and seller in which both agree on the terms and conditions of a sale; also called a *sales contract.*

agricultural property: An unimproved property available for farming activities.

air rights: The right to use, control, and occupy the space above a particular parcel of land.

alienation: A term that means the transfer of title from one person to another.

alienation clause: A provision in a mortgage requiring full payment of the debt upon the transfer of title to the property.

amortization: The repayment of a financial obligation over a period of time in a series of periodic installments; this is the portion of the debt service that reduces the principal.

amortized loan: A financial debt that is paid off over a period of time by a series of periodic payments; a loan can be fully amortized (with equal payments over time) or partially amortized (requiring a balloon payment to satisfy the debt at the end of the term).

anchor tenant: A well-known commercial business such as a chain store or department store used as the primary tenant in a shopping center.

annual percentage rate (APR): The yearly cost of credit.

appeals board: The municipal group to which a property owner can protest a tax bill; also called the *board of equalization.*

apportionment: A division of expenses and charges between buyer and seller at the date of closing; normally, the seller pays expenses accrued up to and including the day of closing.

appraisal: An opinion or estimate of value.

appraisal process: A systematic procedure of collecting and analyzing data to reach an opinion of value.

appraisal report: Submitted by the appraiser to support the opinion of value.

appreciation: An increase in value.

appurtenance: Any right or privilege that belongs to and passes with property.

arrears: Not on time; late in making payments or completing work.

as is: A phrase that disclaims any promises or warranties; a person purchasing real estate "as is" takes it in exactly the condition in which it is found.

assessed value: The value placed on property by the tax assessor for the purpose of determining the property tax.

assessment: A value placed on property for the purpose of levying a property tax.

assessor: A tax official who determines the assessed value of property.

assignee: The person receiving a contractual benefit or right.

assignment: (1) The means by which a person transfers contract rights; (2) occurs when the lessee parts with the entire estate, retaining no interest.

assignor: The person transferring a contractual right or benefit.

assumption fee: A charge levied by a lender to a purchaser who takes title to property by assuming an existing mortgage.

assumption of mortgage: A transfer of mortgage obligation from the seller to the purchaser, who becomes personally liable for any deficiencies occurring in a foreclosure sale, with the original borrower being secondarily liable.

authorization to sell: Another name for the listing agreement entered into by the seller and broker determining the rights and responsibilities of both.

balloon payment: The remaining balance at maturity on a loan that has not been completely repaid through periodic payments; once paid, the outstanding balance is zero.

base rent: In percentage leases, this is the minimum due to the landlord.

basis: The value of property for income tax purposes, calculated as original cost plus all capital improvements, minus accrued depreciation.

basis point: There are 100 basis points in 1 percentage point. See *discount points.*

beneficial interest: An equitable title in property.

beneficiary: (1) The lender under a deed of trust; (2) the investor in a real estate investment trust (REIT).

bilateral contract: A contract in which a contract is given for the promise of another; it becomes binding when mutual promises are communicated.

bill of sale: A document used to transform ownership of personal property.

board of equalization: See *appeals board.*

blanket mortgage: A mortgage that covers more then one piece of real estate.

boot: In federal taxation, cash or something else of value given in the exchange of two properties when the value of one is less than the value of the other.

broker: A person acting as an intermediary for another and who, for a fee, offers to perform certain functions, such as those done by real estate brokers or mortgage brokers.

building codes: Ordinances passed by local governments that specify minimum standards of construction for new buildings and major additions to old construction.

building permit: A permit that is required by local governments before a building can be constructed or remodeled.

capital: (1) In economics, a factor of production that includes all physical resources except for land; (2) in finance, a sum of money.

capital gains: The profit realized from the sale of property or other asset.

capital gains tax: A tax on profits of a qualified capital asset.

capitalization: Conversion of future income into present (current) value; used in the income approach to value.

capitalization rate: The rate of interest considered to be a reasonable return on investment, given the risk.

cash flow: The sum of money generated from income-producing property after all operating expenses and mortgage payments have been made.

certificate of title: A document given by the title examiner stating the quality of title the seller possesses.

chattels: See *personal property*.

close of escrow: See *closing*.

closed mortgage: A mortgage that cannot be prepaid before maturity.

closing: This is the event at which title normally passes and prorations are adjusted between buyer and seller in a real estate transaction; also called *settlement* or *close of escrow*.

closing costs: The expenses incurred and paid at the time of settlement on the transfer of property.

closing date: Date for transferring title of property.

closing statement: A statement indicating debits and credits due on closing.

cloud on title: Any claim affecting title to property.

collateral: Pledged property as security for a loan.

commercial banks: The largest financial intermediary directly involved in the financing of real estate; their primary real estate activity involves short-term loans.

commercial property: Income property zoned for commercial uses such as office buildings or service facilities.

commission: (1) The fee due for a broker's performance, usually a percentage of the sale price; (2) in government, a board empowered to do something.

commitment letter: A promise received from a lender to supply financing if certain conditions are met.

community unit plan: See *planned-unit development.*

comparable: Substantially equivalent property, recently sold, that is used to determine the market value of another property in the market data approach.

comparative analysis: A method of appraising property in which the selling prices of similar properties are used as the basis for estimating the value of the subject property.

comparative square foot method: A technique to estimate reproduction or replacement cost that measures the total square footage or cubic footage and multiplies this total by the current cost per square foot for construction of such a property.

comparison method: A technique for deriving a capitalization rate based on determining how much more an investor has to be compensated for a particular real estate investment in comparison to an "ideal" real estate investment.

compound interest: Interest paid on interest, in addition to being paid on the original principal.

condemnation: The process of exercising eminent domain through court action.

conditional sales contract: A contract for the sale of personal property in which title is retained by the seller until the conditions of the contract have been met.

condominium: A legal form of ownership that involves a separation of property into individual ownership elements and common ownership elements.

confirmation of sale: The court's approval of price, terms, and conditions of a sale ordered by the court.

consideration: Anything of value offered to induce someone to enter into a contractual agreement.

construction loan: A mortgage loan that provides the funds necessary for the building or construction of a real estate project.

constructive eviction: Occurs when the tenant's use of the premises is substantially disturbed or interfered with by the landlord's actions or failure to act.

constructive notice: Under the law, the knowledge a person has about a particular fact irrespective of whether the person knows about the fact or not.

contingency: A term that refers to a variable that may allow a party in a contract to terminate it. As a mortgage contingency, the clause would state that the purchase is contingent for a buyer to obtain a mortgage from a lender to purchase the property. If, after making this attempt, the purchaser finds that he cannot obtain a mortgage, the purchaser will have the right to notify the seller of this contingency not being met and receive their earnest money returned with no further obligation under the contract.

conventional mortgage: A loan made without any government agency guaranteeing or insuring the mortgage.

conveyance: The transfer of title to property from one party to another.

cooperative: A form of property ownership in which a corporation is established to hold title in property and to lease the property to shareholders in the corporation.

cost approach: A method of estimating value based on the economic principle of substitution; the value of a building cannot be greater than the cost of purchasing a similar site and constructing a building of equal utility.

cost basis: The value of property for accounting purposes; equal to the original price plus all acquisition expenses.

co-tenants: A co-owner of a property interest or estate.

date of appraisal: The date as of which the opinion of value is based.

debit: Money owed.

debit coverage ratio: A ratio that is calculated by dividing the annual net operating income by the annual debt service of a mortgage loan.

debt financing: The use of borrowed funds to make a real estate purchase.

debt service: An installment payment that includes both interest and amortization of principal.

declining-balance depreciation: An accelerated depreciation method in which, after the depreciation is taken, the remaining depreciable balance is the base for calculating the subsequent year's depreciation.

decree of foreclosure: A court order making a foreclosure effective.

deduction: A legal adjustment to reduce taxable income.

deed: A written instrument, usually under a seal, that contains an agreement to transfer some property interest from a grantor to a grantee.

deed in lieu of foreclosure: Used by the mortgagor who is in default to convey the property to the mortgage lender in order to eliminate the need for a foreclosure.

deed in trust: Used to convey property to a trustee in a land trust.

deed of release: Given by lienholders, remaindermen, or mortgagees to relinquish their claims on the property.

deed of surrender: Used to merge a life estate with a reversion or remainder.

deed of trust: A deed to real property that serves the same purpose as a mortgage, but involving three parties instead of two; the third party holds title for the benefit of the lender.

default: The failure to perform a contractual obligation or duty.

defect in title: Any lien, claim, or encumbrance on a particular piece of real estate that has been properly recorded in the public records; recorded defects impair clear title and may result in the title being unmarketable.

deferred interest mortgage: Under this mortgage, a lower interest rate and thus a lower monthly mortgage payment is charged; when the property is sold, the lender receives the deferred interest plus a fee for postponing the interest that would normally have been paid each month.

deferred maintenance: Needed repairs that have not been made.

deficiency judgment: A personal claim based on a judicial order against the debtor; this occurs when a property fails to bring in a price at the foreclosure sale that covers the mortgage amount.

depreciation: A decrease in value due to physical deterioration, or functional or economic obsolescence

depreciation (tax): A deduction, based on some percentage of the building value that is used to reduce the tax liability of an owner of qualified property.

deterioration: A loss in value due to wear and tear, by actions of the natural elements or use.

discounted cash flow: See *internal rate of return.*

discounting: The process of adjusting a sum to take into account the time value of money.

discount points: A fee charged by the lender at settlement that results in increasing the lender's effective yield on the money borrowed; one discount point equals 1 percent of the loan amount.

down payment: The amount paid by the purchaser that, when added to the mortgage amount, equals the total sales price; at the time of closing, this is referred to as *equity.*

due diligence: Research and analysis of a company or organization done in preparation for a business transaction (as a corporate merger or purchase of securities).

due diligence clause: Allows a stated period of time in which to inspect the property physically, for zoning, traffic pattern, development, financing, environmental audit, or whatever the purchaser desires before you fully commit to the agreement.

earnest money: A sum of money given to bind an offer of agreement.

easement: A right to limited use of enjoyment by one or more persons in the land of another.

easement appurtenant: An easement created to benefit a particular tract of land.

easement by implication: An easement of necessity, such as the conveyance of a landlocked property to allow a driveway.

easement in gross: A personal right to use the land of another.

economic base analysis: A technique by which a relationship is determined between basic and nonbasic industries to forecast future economic growth in the community.

economic life: The time period over which an improvement to land earns more income than the cost incurred in generating the income.

economic obsolescence: A loss in value due to factors outside the subject property, such as changes in competition or surrounding land use. Also referred to as *locational obsolescence.*

economic rent: The amount of rent that a building could command in an open, competitive market, versus income actually received under a lease agreement.

effective gross income: Income received from the property before the deductions for operating expenses; also called *gross income.*

effective interest rate: The percentage rate of interest actually being paid by a borrower.

eminent domain: The right of government to acquire property for a public purpose after paying just compensation.

encroachment: The extension of some improvement or object across the boundary of an adjoining tract.

encumbrance: Any interest in or claim on the land of another that in some manner burdens or diminishes the value of the property.

Environmental Protection Agency (EPA): The federal agency that oversees and enforces federally enacted minimum standards dealing with environmental protection.

equitable title: The right to obtain absolute ownership to property when legal title is held in another's name.

equity: The interest or value that an owner has in property over and above any indebtedness.

escalation clause: (1) In finance, permits the lender to raise the interest rate upon the occurrence of certain stipulated conditions; (2) in leasing, permits the lessor to raise lease payments upon the occurrence of certain stipulated conditions.

escrow: The process by which money and/or documents are held by a disinterested third person until satisfaction of the terms and conditions of the escrow instructions (as prepared by the parties to the escrow) has been achieved.

escrow agent: An independent third party bound to carry out the written provisions of an escrow agreement.

estoppel: The prevention of a person's denying or alleging a fact contrary to a previous denial or affirmation.

exclusive agency listing: The owner employs only one broker but retains the right to personally sell the property and thereby not pay a commission; however, if anyone other than the owner makes the sale, the listing broker is still entitled to the commission stipulated.

exclusive right-to-sell listing: Under this listing arrangement the broker employed is entitled to a commission no matter who sells the property during the listing period.

Federal Deposit Insurance Corporation (FDIC): A federal agency established to insure the deposits in member commercial banks.

Federal Savings and Loan Insurance Corporation (FSLIC): An agency of the federal government that insures the deposits in member savings and loan associations.

fiduciary: A relationship that implies a position of trust or confidence wherein one person is usually entrusted to hold or manage property or money for another; a fiduciary (an attorney or broker, for example) must carry out the duties in a manner that best serves the interest of the party for whom the fiduciary relationship is established.

financing: Acquisition of borrowed capital.

first lien: A claim with highest priority against property; also known as a *senior lien.*

first mortgage: A mortgage on real estate in which the first lender's rights are superior to the rights of subsequent lenders.

first right of refusal: A provision requiring an owner to allow a specified person or group the first chance to purchase property at a fair market price before it can be offered to a third party; commonly used in condominiums and cooperatives.

flat lease: One where the rent payment remains the same throughout the term of the lease.

flexible loan insurance program (FLIP): A financing technique in which cash is deposited in a pledged, interest-bearing savings account where it serves as both cash collateral for the lender and a source of supplemental payments for the borrower during the first few years of the loan. This occurs when a buyer secures stocks, bonds, or a mortgage on another property with his lender rather than actual cash. The lender has that security pledge in case of a default so he can then cash in or foreclose if necessary.

floor area ratio (FAR): Indicates the relationship between a building area and the land on which it's sited. For example, a 2:1 FAR means that two square feet of floor space may be constructed on one square foot of land.

foreclosure: A legal proceeding that bars a mortgagor's right of redeeming a mortgaged estate or other lien.

front foot: A property measurement for purposes of valuation that is measured by the front footage on the street line.

fully amortized mortgage: A method of loan repayment in which the dollar amount of each payment is the same; the first part of each payment is interest and the remainder reduces the principal (remaining amount owed); over the life of the mortgage, the outstanding balance is reduced to zero.

functional obsolescence: A loss in value due to conditions within the structure that make the building outdated when compared with a new building.

future interest: A person's present right to an interest in real property that will not result in possession or enjoyment until some time in the future; for example, a remainder following a life estate.

gap financing: A loan covering the time period between when the construction loan is due and the conditions set by the permanent lender have not been met.

general warranty deed: Contains covenants in which the grantor formally guarantees that good and marketable title is being conveyed.

gentrification: The process of renewal and rebuilding accompanying the influx of middle-class or affluent people into deteriorating areas that often displaces earlier usually poorer residents.

grandfather clause: An exemption from application of a new law due to previously existing circumstances.

grantee: The purchaser or donee receiving title to property.

grantor: The owner making conveyance of title or interest in the property.

gross income: The actual income received from property before the deduction for any expenses.

gross income multiplier (GIM): A method of appraising income-producing property based on a multiple of the annual gross income; also called *gross rent multiplier.*

gross leasable area: The total area on which rent is paid by tenants.

gross lease: A lease in which the landlord, not the tenant, is responsible for property tax, maintenance, repairs, and other operating costs.

gross rent multiplier: See *gross income multiplier.*

ground lease: A lease of land, usually for a long term.

ground rent: A payment made by the tenant under a ground lease.

housing codes: Local government codes that specify minimum standards that a dwelling unit must meet.

improved land: Any land to which improvements such as roads or buildings have been made.

income approach: A traditional means of appraising property based on the annual net income expected to be produced by the property during its remaining useful life.

income property: Property that generates income for its owner; for example, an office building or apartment complex.

increasing and decreasing returns: This economic principle states that the addition of more factors of production will add higher and higher amounts to net income up to a certain point, which is the point where the maximum value of the asset has been reached; any further addition of factors of production will do nothing to increase the value.

incurable depreciation: Elements of a structure that are neither physically possible nor economically feasible to correct.

independent contractor: One who is not under the direction or control of others and whose time and effort is self-regulated.

installment sale: A means of deferring the paying of capital gains taxes until the installment payments are actually received.

insurance coverage: The total amount of insurance protection carried.

interest reserve: A budgetary amount the bank adds to your debt every month.

internal rate of return: Equating the work of future benefits to the present worth of the investment; also referred to as *discounted cash flow*.

junior mortgage: See *second mortgage*.

land lease: In certain parts of the country, the land under residential real estate is leased through a long-term lease agreement, whereby the owner of the land receives periodic rent for the use of the land.

landlocked: Completely shut in by adjoining parcels of land with no access to public roads.

landlord: The owner or lessor of property.

land trust: A device whereby property is transferred to a trustee under a trust agreement.

latent defect: A defect that cannot be discovered by ordinary inspection.

lease: An agreement by which a landlord gives the right to a tenant to use and to have exclusive possession (but not ownership) of realty for a specified period of time in exchange for the payment of rent.

leased fee: The landlord's interest in leased property.

leasehold: The interest that the tenant has created by a lease.

lease purchase agreement: An arrangement whereby part of the rent payment is applied to the purchase price and when the prearranged total amount has been paid, title is transferred.

legal description: A written description of a parcel of land that locates it precisely.

lessee: Tenant.

lessor: Landlord.

leverage: To use borrowed money to finance the purchase of real estate or other assets.

levy: (1) The imposition of property tax; (2) when executing on a lien, obtaining money by the sale of property.

license: A personal privilege to go upon the land of another; not considered an interest in land.

licensee: Anyone, either a broker or salesperson, licensed to broker real estate.

lien: A legally recognized right to enforce a claim or charge on the property of another for payment of some debt, duty, or obligation.

lienee: The person whose property is burdened by the lien.

life estate: Any estate in real or personal property that is limited in duration to the life of its owner or the life of some other designated person.

like-kind property: Property that qualifies for a tax-free exchange for another property.

limited partnership: An entity with a general partner and one or more passive investors, called limited partners.

line of credit: The extent that an individual may borrow from a bank without further need for approval.

listing contract: An employment agreement between an owner and broker defining the duties and rights of both parties.

loan closing: When all conditions have been met, the loan officer disburses funds and authorizes the recording of the mortgage.

loan commitment: A contractual agreement from a lender to finance a certain amount of the purchase price.

loan correspondent: A person who negotiates and services loans for out-of-state lenders.

loan origination fee: A charge incurred by a borrower to cover the administrative costs of the lender in making the loan.

loan processing: Steps taken by a lender to complete a loan transaction.

loan-to-value ratio: The relationship between the amount borrowed and the appraised value of the property.

location: (1) A particular place that is defined by legal description; (2) how a particular site relates to a surrounding land use pattern.

locational obsolescence: See *economic obsolescence.*

long-term capital gain: The gain realized from the sale or exchange of an asset that has been held for more then one year.

market: The economic function of bringing buyers and sellers together.

market data approach: An approach to research that compares similar property in the same geographic region.

market value: The most probable price a property should bring in a competitive and open market under all conditions requisite to a fair sale; the price at which a willing buyer and a willing seller agree upon, where neither is under any undue pressure and both are negotiating with complete knowledge of the market.

misrepresentation: A misstatement of a fact that is relied upon by the other party.

month-to-month tenancy: A lease that has a term of one month but is renewable for a successive month at the option of both parties.

mortgage: A financing obligation in which the mortgagor (borrower) agrees to pledge property to secure the debt represented by the promissory note or bond.

mortgage banker: A financial middleman who, in addition to bringing borrower and lender together, makes loans, packages them, and sells the packages to investors.

mortgage broker: A person who brings together the user of capital (borrower) and the supplier of capital (lender); for this service, a finder's fee is usually paid by the borrower.

mortgage correspondent: A person authorized to represent a financial institution in a particular geographic area for the purpose of making loans.

mortgagee: A lender who receives a pledge of property to secure a debt.

mortgagee in possession: A lender who has taken over property after default for the purpose of collecting rents and conserving the property until foreclosure.

mortgagor: The borrower, or one who pledges the real estate as security for the loan.

narrative appraisal: The report compiled by an appraiser stating an opinion of value based on data and the appraisal methods used in deriving the estimate of value.

net income: Gross income less all operating expenses; also called *net operating income* (NOI).

net leasable area: The part of a leased area that is exclusively used by a tenant, normally excluding such areas as hallways, laundry rooms, and so on.

net lease: Imposes on the lessee an obligation to pay such costs as property taxes, special assessments, and insurance premiums as agreed to between the parties.

net listing: The broker agrees to sell the property in order to achieve a net price to the owner and anything that is received above the net price is the broker's commission; prohibited by law in many states.

net operating income: See *net income.*

nominal interest rate: The rate of interest stated in the contract.

nonrecourse loan: The sole security for such a loan is the property pledged and, on the basis of agreement, the borrower cannot be held personally responsible.

obsolescence: A loss in value because of a decrease in the usefulness of property due to decay, changes in technology, or people's behavior patterns and tastes.

occupancy: The physical possession of real estate.

occupancy rate: The ratio of the space rented to the total amount of space available for rent.

offer: A promise made by one party, requesting something in exchange for that promise.

offer and acceptance: The necessary elements of mutual assent; for example, an agreement of one party to buy and another party to sell.

open-end mortgage: A loan containing a clause that allows the mortgagor to borrow additional money without rewriting the mortgage.

open listing: An agreement between an owner and a broker giving the broker the nonexclusive right to sell the property.

open mortgage: A mortgage without a prepayment clause.

operating expenses: Expenses incurred in the day-to-day operation of property that are subtracted from gross income to derive net income.

option: A right that is given to a party (optionee) by a property owner (optionor) to purchase or lease property within a specified time, at a specified price and terms.

overimproved land: Occurs when the owner puts more money into improvements to the land than can be profitably absorbed.

participation mortgage: An agreement between a mortgagee and a mortgagor that provides the lender with a certain percentage of ownership in the project after the lender makes the loan.

partition: The dividing of real estate held by two or more people that results in each of the parties holding individual or severalty (more than one person) ownership.

percentage lease: Commonly used for commercial property; for example, a shopping mall, where rent for the space is based on the tenant's gross sales at the premises.

personal property: Moveable items that are not annexed to or part of the land; also referred to as *chattels*.

physical deterioration: The loss in value due to wear and tear of the structure.

physical life: The normal or expected time over which an asset such as a building should last.

planned-unit development (PUD): A type of exception or special-use permitted under many modern zoning ordinances that allows a mixture of different land uses or densities; also referred to as a *community unit plan.*

plat: A map showing the division of land into lots and blocks.

plat books: Located in public records, these books identify parcels of property that have been subdivided into lots and blocks.

points: See *discount points.*

population density: The number of people in a given area.

prepaid expenses: Payments made by the purchaser at settlement to pay for future charges such as property taxes and mortgage insurance.

prepayment clause: A section in a mortgage note that permits the borrower to pay without penalty the outstanding balance before the due date.

prepayment penalty: The charge levied by the lender for paying off a mortgage prior to its maturity date; also called a *yield maintenance penalty.*

prescription: See *adverse possession.*

prescriptive easement: An easement obtained by the open, hostile, and continuous use of the property belonging to someone else for the statutory period of time.

present value: The worth in today's dollars of a future income stream and/or reversion at a given discount rate.

price: An amount usually expressed in terms of money paid for property.

primary financing: The loan that has the first priority.

prime rate: The interest rate charged to a lender's AAA customers; this is normally the base from which other interest rates are derived.

principal: The main parties to a transaction; for example, the buyer and seller are principals in the purchase of real property.

procuring cause: The actions by a broker that result in the owner being able to make a sale.

promissory note: An unconditional written promise of one person to pay a certain sum of money to another at a future specified time.

purchase and leaseback: The simultaneous buying of property and leasing it back to the seller.

purchase money mortgage: A mortgage given by the seller to the buyer to cover all or part of the sales price.

rate of return: A percentage relationship between the investment price or equity invested and the composite return.

Real Estate Investment Trust (REIT): A method of pooling investment money using the trust form of ownership; offers some of the flow-through tax advantages of a partnership while retaining many of the attributes and advantages of a corporate operation.

Real Estate Settlement Procedures Act (RESPA): A law that covers most mortgage loans made on one- to four-unit residential properties; requires the lender to provide the loan applicant with pertinent information so that the borrower can make informed decisions as to which lender will be used to finance the purchase.

redemption period: The right of a mortgagor to make good on a loan default within a specified time and thereby reclaim the property.

refinancing: An extension or restructuring of the existing financing either through the same lender or through a new financial arrangement.

release clause: A stipulation that, upon the payment of a certain percentage of a loan, certain portions of the collateral will be removed from the blanket lien held by the lender.

remainder: The right of future possession and use that goes to someone other than the grantor upon termination of a life estate.

remainderman: The person who is to receive possession of the property after the death of a life tenant.

renegotiable rate mortgage: A loan in which the maturity is fixed (for example, thirty years) but the interest rate, and hence the monthly payment, is renegotiated periodically (for example, every three or five years).

rent: The payment made for the use of property.

rent concession: A discount lowering the actual cost of a lease to a tenant.

rent control: Refers to laws in certain geographic locations that impose limitations on how much rent can be charged and what percentage increase can be levied by the landlord.

replacement cost: The cost of substituting a similar structure with utility equivalent to the subject property but constructed with modern materials.

reversion: The right of future possession and use by the grantor of a life estate.

right of first refusal: The right to the first opportunity to lease or purchase real property; for example, apartment tenants might retain the right of first refusal when their units are being converted to condominiums.

right of way: An easement allowing someone to cross over a parcel of land.

run with the land: A phrase describing rights or covenants that bind or benefit successive owners of a property; certain restrictions, easements, and covenants are part of the ownership of land and thus are not terminated when title is transferred but remain in effect from owner to owner.

sale-leaseback: A technique used by owners of property as a means of raising capital; involves the simultaneous selling and leasing back of the property, usually through a net lease.

sales contract: See *agreement of sale.*

second mortgage: A mortgage subordinate to a first mortgage; also referred to as a *junior mortgage.*

security deposit: A sum of money given to assure the performance of an obligation.

senior lien: See *first lien.*

setback lines: A requirement in zoning ordinances in which all structures are to be a minimum distance from property lines.

settlement: See *closing.*

settler: See *trustor.*

sheriff's sale: See *tax sale.*

specific performance: An equitable remedy in which the court orders the contract to be performed as agreed to by the parties.

straight-line depreciation: A method of computing depreciation for income tax purposes in which the difference between the original cost and the salvage value is deducted in installments, evenly over the depreciable life of the asset.

straight-term mortgage: See *term mortgage.*

strict foreclosure: After a delinquent borrower has been notified and the proper papers have been filed, the court designates a specific period during which the balance of the default must be paid in full; if the payment is not made, the borrower's rights are waived and the court awards full legal title to the lender.

sublease: The transfer of a lease from the original lessee to a sublessee wherein the original lessee retains a reversion; the original lessee remains directly liable to the lessor for the rent, which is usually paid by the sublessee to the lessee and then from the lessee to the lessor.

survey: The process by which a parcel of land is measured.

take-out commitment: An agreement by a permanent lender to provide the long-term financing for a real estate project when a certain event occurs, normally the completion of the project.

taxation: The process by which a government raises monies to fund its operation.

tax base: The total tax-assessed value of all real property in a particular area.

tax certificate: A document given to the purchaser at a tax sale auction that entitles the holder to a tax deed or a treasurer's deed at the end of the tax redemption period. Every taxing body allows a redemption period (with penalties and interest, of course) for late payment of real estate taxes. This allows the owner every opportunity to reinstate himself.

tax deed: A deed issued when property is sold to satisfy delinquent taxes.

tax-free exchanges: A method of deferring capital gains taxes by exchanging one qualified property for another qualified property.

tax rate: The rate, normally stated in units of $100, multiplied by the assessed value of property to determine the amount of the property tax due.

tax roll: Located in the public records, this identifies each parcel of land, the owner of record, and the assessed value of the property.

tax sale: Foreclosure of an unpaid tax lien in a public sale. Also called a *sheriff's sale.*

tax shelter: A phrase often used to describe some of the tax advantages of real estate or other investments that shield income or gains from income tax liability.

tenancy: The possession of an estate.

tenancy at sufferance: A tenancy that is created when one is in wrongful possession of realty, even though the original possession may have been legal.

tenancy in common: A form of concurrent ownership where two or more persons hold separate titles in the same estate.

tenancy in partnership: A multiple form of ownership where the property is held in a lawful business venture.

tenant: One who has the legal right to occupy or hold property; most often refers to someone who occupies the property of another under an agreement to pay rent.

tenement: Property held by a tenant.

term mortgage: A method of financing in which only interest is paid during the time of the loan; at maturity, generally five years or less, the entire principal is due; also referred to as a *straight-term mortgage.*

time value of money: The idea that because money is assumed to earn interest, holding one dollar today is considered to be more valuable than holding one dollar a year from today.

title: The legally recognized evidence of a person's right to possess property.

title company: A company that examines the public records to determine the marketability of an owner's title.

title insurance: A policy that protects the insured against loss or damage due to defects in title.

topographic map: A map showing changes in elevation through contour lines.

topography: A description of surface features of land.

trading on the equity: Increasing the rate of return on the owner's equity by borrowing part or all of the purchase price at a rate of interest less than the expected rate of return generated on the net income of the property.

trust agreement: An arrangement whereby legal title to property is transferred by the grantor (or trustor) to a person called a trustee, to be held and managed by that person for the benefit of another, called a beneficiary.

trustee: (1) One who holds property in trust for another and is charged with the duty to protect, preserve, and enhance the value and best use of the trust property; (2) one who holds property in trust for another to secure the performance of an obligation.

trustor: The person who creates a trust and gives the instructions to the trustee; also called a *settler*.

underimproved land: A parcel of land that can profitably absorb more units than are currently being employed.

undisclosed principal: The unknown person for which a real estate agent is acting.

undivided interest: The interest of co-owners in which individual interest is indistinguishable.

uninsurable title: A title that a title insurance company refuses to insure due to some present claim or encumbrance against it.

utility: (1) The usefulness or satisfaction received from a good or service; (2) various services such as electricity, water, and gas.

waiver: The renunciation of a claim or privilege.

warranty: An assurance that defects do not exist.

warranty deed: A deed in which the grantor makes formal assurance as to the quality of title.

water table: The distance from ground level to natural groundwater.

wear and tear: The lessening in value of an asset due to ordinary and normal use.

wraparound mortgage: A second mortgage that provides an owner additional capital without the owner needing to refinance the first mortgage.

yield: The interest earned by an investor on the investment.

yield maintenance penalty: See *prepayment penalty.*

yield to maturity: The total return to the investor if the investment is held for the full term.

zoning: The regulation of structures and uses of property within designated districts or zones, including such elements as lot sizes, types of structures permitted, building heights, setbacks, and density.

zoning ordinance: A zoning law passed by a local government that consists of a text of regulations and a map.

Phone Call to Owners
of Real Estate

When you are aggressively searching for properties that are candidates for flipping, you will have a big advantage if you can find properties that are not already widely advertised as being for sale. Here is a sample telephone script to use when approaching the owner of a property you are interested in:

"Hello, Mr./Ms. Owner. My name is _____. Do you own the property located at 1617 South Southport? Have you thought of selling the property?"

If the answer is no: "Do you plan on selling any time in the near future? When?" *Make sure to mark your calendar for follow-up calls.* "Thank you very much for your time. I will be in touch from time to time."

If the answer is yes, it's extremely important for you to respond professionally and sound as if you have been buying real estate all your life. Ask the following questions:

- Why are you considering selling now?
- How long have you thought about selling?

- How long have you owned the property?
- How many units comprise the property?
- What are the real estate taxes?
- What is your mortgage balance?
- Who pays the expenses?
- Is the property tenant-heated (does the tenant pay the utilities for heat and air conditioning)?
- Do you have a management company managing the property?
- Do you have any partners?
- Have you discussed selling the property with your [partner/spouse]?
- Have you had a recent appraisal of the property?
- What do you feel the property is worth?
- How did you arrive at that value?

"I would like the opportunity to meet you personally and inspect the property. I happen to have an appointment in the area of your property on ___ at ___ A.M./P.M. Are you available at ___ A.M./P.M. that same day?

"I will be sending you a letter requesting income and expense information that I'll require in order to analyze your property properly. What is your present mailing address? I look forward to meeting you on _____."

Letter Asking for Additional Information

I f you're considering buying a property to flip, you need to know a lot more about it than just its present value. The following is a sample letter to write to the owner of a property you may be interested in buying.

August 23, 2003

Mr./Ms. Owner of Record
555 Your Favorite Street
Los Angeles, CA 90004

Re: 1111 W. Montrose Avenue, Chicago, IL 60613

Dear Mr./Ms. Owner:

It was a pleasure talking to you the other day regarding the marketing of your property as referenced above.

When we meet, it would be extremely helpful if you could have prepared the following current information:

1. Property survey and lot size
2. Number of apartments and number of rooms per apartment
3. Rentals charged to tenants and copies of any and all leases, and security deposit information
4. Year-to-date annual operating expenses for the following items:
   a. Real estate taxes
   b. Electric
   c. Gas
   d. Management
   e. Trash service
   f. Maintenance and repair costs
   g. Water
   h. Advertising costs
   i. Janitor wages
   j. Insurance cost
   k. Decorating costs
   l. Any other fees itemized
   m. Phase-one environmental audit
5. Mortgage:
   a. Original amount and date
   b. Interest rate and term

I look forward to meeting you on September 3, 2003 at 2:30 P.M.

Very truly yours,

Mark B. Weiss

Appendix C

Annual Property Operating Data

ere is a sample form you might use in determining the income and expenses you could expect from a residential rental property if you were to purchase it and hold it for a period of time. Making a detailed analysis like this is an essential step before buying any property that you may end up holding.

Yearly Amount

SCHEDULED RENTAL INCOME

5% vacancy

Other income: laundry, vending, etc.

GROSS OPERATING INCOME

Accounting and legal

Advertising

Decorating

Electric

Elevator

Exterminating

Gas

Insurance

Janitorial

Landscaping

Management

Miscellaneous

Real estate taxes

Repairs and maintenance

Scavenger

Sewer and water

Supplies

Taxes: workers' compensation/state and federal withholding

TOTAL EXPENSES

Gross operating income

Total expenses

Net operating income

Example of a Contract Rider

When purchasing a property, be sure to include in the purchase contract any contingencies that you might later need. These clauses can serve as legitimate reasons for canceling the contract if problems with the property become apparent. It is also important to spell out the responsibility that each party to the contract has for any items that will be transferred along with the property, such as payment of taxes.

Rider to contract dated June 30, 2003
for the purchase of 525 W. Roscoe, Chicago, Ill.

1. Seller will provide to purchaser for purchaser's approval within ten days copies of the following:
   a. All leases
   b. All service contracts
   c. Copies of all invoices representing expenses in the broker's listing sheet
   d. Survey
   e. Floor plans
   f. 2002 and 2003 real estate tax bills

2. Seller will not enter into any new leases for the property without purchaser's written approval.
3. Seller will provide purchaser with evidence of no environmental hazards contained on or in the property.
4. This contract is subject to approval by purchaser's and seller's attorneys within 10 days of acceptance.
5. Purchaser warrants that the roof, boiler, electrical systems, and all appliances are in good working order and will be so on day of closing.
6. Prior to closing and upon reasonable notice, seller will allow purchaser or purchaser's agent access to the property to prepare for decorating, renovation, or other reasons.
7. This contract is contingent upon a physical inspection by purchaser or purchaser's agent.
8. The 2003 real estate taxes shall be paid by the seller when the actual real estate tax bill shall arrive. The 2004 real estate taxes shall be prorated at 110 percent of the 2003 real estate taxes based on the actual real estate tax bill.

Accepted this day: _____

(Date)

Seller: _____

(Signature)

Purchaser: _____

(Signature)

Notice of Intent to Convert Property to Condominiums

As with just about every major action in real estate, turning a property into condominiums should be preceded by a careful consideration of your legal responsibilities. This is an example of the type of notice you may be legally required to give to any current tenants before making such a change to a property.

NOTICE TO TENANTS
February 13, 2004 via Certified Mail
with Return Receipt Requested

The Undersigned proudly announces that the property at 4028–30 North Sheridan, Chicago, Illinois, will soon become available for condominium ownership. It is the intention of the undersigned to submit the building to the provisions of the Illinois Condominium Property Act. A Declaration of Condominium will be recorded on a date not less than 120 days and not later than one year after the date of this letter.

The Undersigned intends to act in the following manner with respect to residents:

1. Your Lease will be fully honored until its expiration date. It is not our present intention, however, to renew or extend any leases except as provided in this letter.

2. If your Lease expires prior to June 13, 2004, you have the right to extend your tenancy to June 13, 2004 on the same terms and conditions and for the same rental as are now applicable, provided you advise me in writing of your intention to do so within thirty (30) days after receipt of this Notice.

3. If you are over sixty-five years of age, or deaf or blind, or unable to walk without assistance (a special tenant), you will be entitled to extend your tenancy to June 13, 2004, on the same terms and conditions and at the same rental as are now applicable, provided you advise the undersigned in writing of your intention to do so within thirty (30) days after receipt of this Notice.

4. You have a right of first refusal to purchase your unit until April 13, 2004 (or June 13, 2004, if you are a special tenant). You must exercise this right by advising me in writing of your intentions within thirty (30) days after being notified that a purchase contract has been signed for your unit.

This Notice does not in any way relieve you of the obligation to pay rent during the time you are in possession.

All notices required hereunder shall be given by a written notice delivered in person or mailed, certified or registered mail, return receipt requested, to 4028–30 N. Sheridan, L.L.C., Attn: Mark B. Weiss, 2442 North Lincoln Avenue, Chicago, Illinois 60614.

MARK B. WEISS REAL ESTATE BROKERAGE, INC.
as Manager for 4028–30 N. Sheridan, L.L.C.

About the Author

Since 1988, Mark B. Weiss Real Estate Brokerage, Inc. has become well recognized nationally as a leader in the sale of commercial and investment property for financial institutions, private owners, corporations, and trusts, and as a developer of vintage property renovations throughout Chicago's neighborhoods.

A graduate of DePaul University, Mr. Weiss is immediate past president of the Lincoln Park Builder's Club, and a member of the Rogers Park Builders Club and the Edgewater Uptown Builders Club. Mr. Weiss served as a member of the board of directors of the Chicago Association of Realtors from 2000–2003. He served as chairman of the Association's Commercial Committee from 2000–2002. Mr. Weiss is a member and past director of the Illinois C.C.I.M. Chapter, the Chicago Real Estate Council, the National Association of Realtors, the Realtors National Marketing Institute, the Real Estate Investment Association, the National Association of Bankruptcy Trustees, the National Association of Auctioneers, the International Council of Shopping Centers, the Lincoln Park Chamber of Commerce, and the Andersonville Chamber of Commerce. Mr. Weiss has been awarded continuously since 2000 "Good Neighbor Awards" from the Chicago Association of Realtors for excellence in vintage renovation of historical properties in Chicago's many neighborhoods. Because of his celebrity and expertise in the field of real estate, Mr. Weiss often appears on television programs as a real estate expert for interviews and panel discussions and is consulted as a "go-to guy," often quoted in the *Chicago Sun Times*, *Chicago Magazine*, *The Chicago Tribune*, *Woman's World Magazine*, and *Realtor Publications*, as well as other newspapers and national publications.

Mr. Weiss is the author of *Streetwise® Landlording and Property Management* and *The Everything® Homebuying Book, Second Edition*, published by Adams Media, and *Condos, Townhomes, and Co-Ops*, published by Dearborn Publishing.

Index